Wome

Margaret C. Ives was, until recently, head of the Department of German at the University of Lancaster. Since 1989 she has also been a Reader in the Diocese of Blackburn and is a regular preacher and discussion group leader at St Paul's Church, Scotforth, Lancaster.

Women of the Passion

The Women of the New Testament tell their stories

Margaret C. Ives

*with illustrations by
Gillian Bell-Richards
and meditations by
Ruth Tiller*

CANTERBURY
PRESS
Norwich

Text © Margaret C. Ives
Illustrations © Gillian Bell-Richards
Meditations entitled 'In the Hill Country', 'A Sign that will be
Spoken Against', 'Martha, Mary and the Lord', 'The Samaritan
Woman', 'Via Dolorosa', 'Who Touched
Me?' and 'The Widow's Mite' © Ruth Tiller 1998

First published in 1998 by The Canterbury Press Norwich
(a publishing imprint of Hymns Ancient & Modern Limited,
a registered charity)
St Mary's Works, St Mary's Plain,
Norwich, Norfolk NR3 3BH

Margaret Ives has asserted her right under the Copyright, Designs and
Patents Act 1988, to be identified as Author of this Work

British Library Cataloguing in Publication Data

A catalogue record for this book is available
from the British Library

ISBN 1-85311-237-2

*Typeset by Rowland Phototypesetting Ltd,
Bury St Edmunds, Suffolk
Printed in Great Britain by Biddles Ltd,
Guildford and King's Lynn*

Contents

Women of the Way – *Pentecost and Ordinary
    Time*

Introduction

A number of women were also present, watching
from a distance; they had followed Jesus from Galilee
and looked after him.

(Matthew 27:55)

In their accounts of the Passion of Our Lord, all four
Gospels mention the women who stationed themselves at
the foot of the Cross to keep a last vigil during Christ's
suffering. Some are known to us by name: Mary of
Magdala, Mary the mother of James and Joseph, Salome,
and that very special Mary who had been chosen to bear
the Christ-child in her womb. Some are anonymous:
Mark's Gospel refers to 'many others who had come up
to Jerusalem with him' (Mark 15:41). A close reading of
the Passion narratives reveals that there were also one or
two more, not necessarily from Galilee, who had a part to
play in the unfolding drama: Martha and Mary at Bethany,
the maidservants in the High Priest's courtyard, Pilate's
wife, the daughters of Jerusalem.

The meditations that follow in this book first arose out
of a study of these Passion narratives, but they were then
extended to include other women who feature in the New
Testament, especially those in the writings of St Luke and

the Epistles of St Paul. They have now been arranged in a sequence designed to follow the pattern of the Christian Year, and it is hoped that as such they can be used for general Bible study or for prayer groups. The more detailed section 'Women of the Passion' could, if wished, serve as a Lent course book or a special Holy Week devotion.

Women of the Mystery

Advent, Christmas and Epiphany

Mary: the Annunciation

Advent 1

In the sixth month the angel Gabriel was sent by God
to Nazareth, a town in Galilee, with a message for a
girl betrothed to a man named Joseph, a descendant
of David; *the girl's name was Mary.*

(Luke 1:26–27)

At the beginning of the Christian year, in Advent, we will
almost certainly hear again the story of the Annunciation.
It is a story so familiar to us, a story depicted in so many
stained-glass windows and on Christmas cards, that we
tend to forget its disturbing aspects and implications.

The angel Gabriel is generally shown surrounded by a
brilliant light; his wings are folded behind him as he
descends into Mary's room, but his halo and face are radi-
ant as he speaks the message of God to her. Mary herself
is often seated at a table or window, gazing at the angel
with rapt attention. There is no doubt much truth in these
depictions, arising, as they do, from the imagination and
artistic skills of devout believers in almost 2,000 years
of Christian history. But can we ever really envisage the
astounding nature of this unique event?

Mary is still quite young, a mere girl, perhaps about fourteen. She is betrothed, that is to say she is 'spoken for', but according to the custom of the time not expecting to be married for another year or so. As she goes about her daily duties within the household perhaps thinking about the future, wondering if she will be strong enough to shoulder the responsibilities of being a wife and mother, suddenly – without any warning – there is a brightness all around her and a Presence which calls her by name and hails her as the one chosen by God to give birth to the promised Messiah. What can it all mean? The angel is not speaking of something that will take place after her wedding to Joseph, but of something that is about to happen to her *now* as the Holy Spirit overshadows her. No wonder she is troubled, perplexed, frightened and bewildered! (Luke 1:29)

When I was a child growing up in a Lincolnshire country village, we used sometimes to play a game in which one girl had to sit in the middle of a circle while the other children danced round her. It was called 'Poor Mary sat weeping on a bright summer's day' and I was always very puzzled as to the meaning of these words. My grandmother explained that they referred to a girl who had lost her sweetheart or husband, since the whole object of the game was for the girl in the middle to seize one of the dancers and change places, but I wondered later if there was not perhaps some much deeper folk-memory at work. In Hebrew the name 'Mary' is derived from a root meaning 'bitter' and, looked at in a certain way, the life of Mary, Mother of Our Lord, was by no means easy. She is first of all 'discovered to be with child', a terrible thing in those

days when an unmarried girl was required to be a virgin
until her wedding (Deuteronomy 22:13–20). Then she has
to watch her child growing up and growing away from
her, as Jesus stays behind in the Temple at Jerusalem to
question the teachers of the Law and later on embarks on
a career as an itinerant preacher, wandering from place to
place, frequently upsetting the religious leaders of the day
and mystifying his friends and family in the process. Finally
she has to see him condemned to death and executed along-
side robbers and outlaws. It is indeed a bitter cup that
is offered her, and ordinary people down the ages have
identified with her heartbreak as her life develops in
unexpectedly strange and puzzling patterns.

What was Mary really like? Many of the great artists
paint her with a slightly wistful expression, but nevertheless an expression of serenity and unquestioning calm.
After the initial shock at the angel's prophecy she does not
argue about her fate, she does not rebel and ask 'Why me?'
Her answer is 'Be it unto me according to thy word.' (AV)
She must know that she will be accused of unchastity, that
she will face humiliation and disgrace, that Joseph will
threaten to 'put her away' and perhaps join those who
point the finger of scorn, but nevertheless she is prepared
to put her faith in God and to do as she is asked. What is
it that gives her such certainty and enables such obedience?
We must remember that she *saw* the angel, that the Holy
Spirit came upon her (Luke 1:35) – that, by a special gift
of grace, something happened to her, a spiritual experience
so profound that she knew beyond any shadow of doubt
that she would be vindicated, that God would see her
through and would not abandon her. It is this vision of

the angel and this unshakeable spiritual conviction that gives her the courage to say yes to enduring the months ahead, the courage to undertake the journey to visit Elizabeth and seek confirmation that both of them are chosen vessels of God's mysterious purpose, the courage later to go with Joseph to Bethlehem, secure in the knowledge that she will be safely delivered and that the Christ-child will be born.

Prayer and reflection

'I am the Lord's servant,' said Mary; 'may it be as you have said' (Luke 1:38). Perhaps if we could see an angel, we too could show such unquestioning obedience. There are indeed even today people who claim to have had such an experience or to have heard the voice of God in other ways, and it is certainly the duty of Christian people to listen continually through prayer and meditation for that 'still, small voice' that seeks to guide our lives. So let us pray that we may be able to hear it and, having heard it, may carry out its commandments.

Heavenly Father, who sent the angel down to Mary and spoke to her through his words, help us too, amid all the distractions of this life, its noise and bustle and its constant demands, to discern what is your will for us and to accept our allotted tasks as Mary accepted hers. Give us that humility of spirit that thinks not of self, but rather of service, and

*enable us to find in obedience to your Word our true
joy and fulfilment.*

In a society where, for many, consumerism is the new
religion, what can we do, during the season of Advent, to
'put Christ back into Christmas' and to make it once again
a holy time of year?

Elizabeth

Advent 2

When his period of duty was completed Zechariah
returned home. *His wife Elizabeth conceived, and for
five months she lived in seclusion*, thinking, 'This is the
Lord's doing; now at last he has shown me favour and
taken away from me the disgrace of childlessness.'

(Luke 1:23–24)

Elizabeth – the name means 'consecrated unto God' – is
the first woman to be mentioned in Luke's Gospel. She
came of a priestly family, for her husband, Zechariah, a
priest descended from Aaron, was only allowed to marry
into a family of similar status, and we are told that both
she and her husband were very devout people. But a great
misfortune had befallen them: they had no children, and
at that time this was considered a terrible disgrace, particularly for the woman. We can therefore understand Elizabeth's desire to live in seclusion for the first five months
of her pregnancy. Even today some women who for years
have longed to have a baby are very reluctant at first to
talk about a successful conception. Can it really be?

Perhaps there is some other, less happy, reason for the bodily signs and changes? Perhaps something will go wrong and the disappointment be all the more unbearable?

We can presume that Elizabeth had some inkling of what was happening to her. Her husband Zechariah, while serving in the Temple, had had a vision that he and his wife were to be blessed with a son, and although he had been struck dumb because he doubted the words of the angel, he could still have written down his experience for his wife and told her to wait in hope. As for Elizabeth, she must surely have thought back to other women in the Old Testament who gave birth late in life: Sarah, the wife of Abraham, who gave birth to Isaac, and Hannah, mother of the prophet Samuel, who prayed so fervently in the Temple for the gift of a child that the priest on duty thought she must be either out of her mind or inebriated (1 Samuel 1:12–18).

Then, after five months, Elizabeth really is sure. She can feel the child moving inside her and can look forward to a live birth, knowing that God's promise, communicated to her husband by the angel, is about to be fulfilled. Final confirmation comes when, a month later, she is visited by her younger cousin Mary who reveals that she, too, has conceived a child in a miraculous and mysterious fashion. As Mary approaches, Elizabeth feels her own child 'leap for joy'. It is a sign that Mary is indeed 'most highly favoured' and that the child that will be born of her will be pure and holy, a manifestation of the Divine, a visitation by the Lord of Creation to his creation to experience all its trials and temptations and to reveal a new pattern by which all of us may live.

The meeting of Elizabeth and Mary is one of the great themes of Western art. In one such depiction, by the Austrian painter Rueland Frueauf the Elder (c. 1445–1507), the two women are holding each other's hands, with Elizabeth's hand gently touching Mary's garment where it swells out over her blossoming figure. The picture captures the mystery of pregnancy, but more than this it shows the awe in which Elizabeth holds Mary, her recognition that both of them are instruments of the Divine. For what a strange meeting it is! For Elizabeth, the disgrace of childlessness is about to be removed, but what is she to make of the fact that her kinswoman Mary is not even married? Elizabeth, however, knows no doubt or hesitation. She has led a pure and devout life and accepts without question that Mary, too, a member of the same God-fearing family, has committed no act of unchastity but has become the chosen vessel of God's power. Secure in this knowledge, she can then exclaim 'God's blessing is on you above all women, and his blessing is on the fruit of your womb' (Luke 1:42) and Mary herself can utter that great song of praise and thanksgiving and prophecy that we now call the Magnificat (Luke 1:46–55).

There is much here that cannot be explained, much that remains a mystery. Some people try very hard to reduce everything to human terms and to cut out the Divine dimension. This is surely wrong. We need the humility to admit that what took place in the hill country of Judaea and at Bethlehem 2,000 years ago was something truly miraculous, a Divine intervention into human history, God coming down to our level that we might be shown the way back to God. We cannot explain every detail of this, nor should we seek to do so, but we do know that it happened because what occurred then and in the years following, as Elizabeth's child John the Baptist and Mary's child Jesus Christ grew to maturity, was so stupendous, so amazing, that the history of the world was decisively altered and we now talk about B C, before Christ, and A D (Anno Domini), the Year of the Lord. Elizabeth and Mary could have raised all kinds of objections to their parts in the divine plan, but their simple faith upheld them: they *believed*.

Prayer and reflection

'My soul doth magnify the Lord', the opening words of the Magnificat, are Mary's words of thanksgiving as she realizes the tremendous privilege bestowed upon her as the one chosen to bear the Son of God. As we prepare ourselves to commemorate Christ's birth at Christmas time, let us, too, reflect on the wonder of this event and the difference it has made to our lives.

> *Dear Lord and Saviour, whose coming we earnestly await during this season of Advent, increase our faith that, like Mary who was chosen to be your mother and Elizabeth, mother of John the Baptist, we may come to know what you would have us do and, like them, be given strength to accomplish it.*

What else might we learn from the Magnificat? What are the implications for the Christian life of its central passage (Luke 1:51−53)?

In the Hill Country

This is a moment of pure happiness,
To be savoured and enjoyed. Time given
Before their lives are turned
Completely up-side down.
Virgin conception and post-menopausal pregnancy
Will, besides the physical discomforts,
Give wagging tongues their fill.

And then these sons of joy
Cannot but bring them turmoil and distress –
Not for these mothers a comfortable pride,
But costly love, watching lives lived
Beyond their choosing.

But now, the music of the spheres
Finds an echo in the rhythm of the womb,
And in that leap of recognition
The blessing is received.

Luke 1:39–45 RT

Mary: the Birth of Jesus

Christmas

> Joseph went up to Judaea from the town of Nazareth
> in Galilee, to register in the city of David called Beth-
> lehem, because he was of the house of David by
> descent; and with him went *Mary, his betrothed* who
> was expecting her child.

> (Luke 2:4–5)

Luke's Gospel does not tell us very much about Joseph.
To find out a little more we have to turn to Matthew where
we read that he was 'a man of principle', someone with
high moral standards. What then must have been his dis-
may on learning that the young woman to whom he was
betrothed had been found to be with child. Yet he does
not condemn, or demand an explanation. 'At the same
time wanting to save her from exposure, Joseph made up
his mind to have the marriage contract quietly set aside'
(Matthew 1:19). Then comes the dream in which the angel
reveals to him that Mary has been chosen for the most
important task ever assigned to a woman, that of bearing
the Messiah, and that he, Joseph, is to be her earthly pro-

tector. By the time they reach Bethlehem, Mary is secure
in this knowledge. No one can mock or revile her, she can
make the journey as a married woman, confidently looking
forward to her confinement.

What will the child look like? This, surely, is every
mother's question as at last, after nine months of waiting,
she is about to see for the first time the tiny being whose
life she has nurtured within her body. There is a lovely
hymn which tries to imagine Mary at this moment:

> For Mary, Mother of Our Lord,
> God's Holy Name be praised,
> Who first the Son of God adored,
> As on her child she gazed.

(100 Hymns for Today, No. 27)

Yet for Mary, as for all mothers, there is something else
that mingles with the joy and wonder of having borne a
healthy child. What will become of him? How will he
develop? What will happen to him when he grows up?
Luke's Gospel further records how the shepherds come to
the manger with the message that this child is to be the
Messiah, the deliverer of his people. 'Mary treasured up
all these things and pondered over them' (Luke 2:19). Perhaps, in the beginning, she had been so overwhelmed by
the appearance of the angel and the overshadowing by the
Holy Spirit that she had had little time to think ahead to
the future. Then, on meeting Elizabeth, there had been a
deep conviction that something was happening to both of
them that was going to have profound repercussions for

the social and political order. Now there is a hint of fore-boding. Deliverance from whatever it might be – political oppression, hunger, sin and evil – cannot come without upheaval, conflict, pain and sacrifice. Mary knows that her child is not going to have an easy life. It will be no surprise to her that when she and Joseph bring the child into the Temple to give thanks for her safe delivery Simeon will recognize him as the one who is to be 'a light that will bring revelation to the Gentiles' (Luke 2:32), but will also say to Mary 'This child is destined to be a sign that will be rejected; and you too will be pierced to the heart' (Luke 2:35).

Prayer and reflection

Christmas is rightly seen as a time of 'tidings of comfort and joy', but the Church calendar also recognizes that Christ's coming into the world caused conflict and dissension. 26 December is the Feast Day of St Stephen, the first Christian martyr, and on 28 December many churches commemorate the Holy Innocents, the male infants put to death by Herod as recounted in Matthew's Gospel (Matthew 2:16–18). The Feast of the Epiphany on 6 January reminds us that one of the gifts offered to the Christ-child was myrrh, foreshadowing his burial in the tomb. Perhaps one of the ways in which we can make Christmas time a more holy time of year is by reflecting on these events and remembering them in our prayers. Particularly on Holy Innocents Day we could pray for all bereaved mothers, who like Rachel, regarded in Old

Testament times as the mother-protector of Israel, seem beyond human comfort.

> A voice was heard in Rama, sobbing in bitter grief; it was Rachel weeping for her children, and refusing to be comforted, because they were no more. (Matthew 2:18)

> *Look mercifully, Lord, we pray, on all mothers who have lost their children: through miscarriage, still birth, cot death, or childhood illness; through accident or misadventure or violent crime; through famine or natural disaster. Be with them in their grief and bewilderment, console them in their suffering, and give them the assurance that even the shortest life is of value in the Divine scheme of things and that nothing precious is ever lost in your sight. In this way, Lord, help them once again to face the future with courage and with hope.*

What can we do to help those for whom the Christmas season is a sad and difficult time? How can we try to comfort the bereaved, especially bereaved mothers grieving for their children? How sensitive are we to their feelings?

Anna the Prophetess

Epiphany

*There was also a prophetess, Anna the daughter of
Phanuel, of the tribe of Asher.* She was a very old
woman, who had lived seven years with her husband
after she was first married, and then alone as a widow
to the age of eighty-four. She never left the temple,
but worshipped night and day with fasting and
prayer.

(Luke 2:36–37)

Simeon was not the only person who greeted the Christ-
child when he was brought into the Temple, but Anna,
unlike Simeon, made no eloquent speech of welcome or,
if she did, her words have not been recorded. For this
reason she remains an obscure figure: there are few depictions of her in art.

Yet what we do know about her is highly significant.
First of all, she was very old and had been a widow for a
very long time (if we assume that she was married about
the age of 14, then at least for 60 years). Her life during
her widowhood had been one of chastity and abstinence,

marked by prayer and fasting, devoted entirely to the service of God. Why had she made this decision? It could be that her seven years of married life had been so happy – or perhaps so traumatic – that, on the death of her husband, she had no wish to remarry and had chosen the religious life as the only available alternative. Having made her decision, however, she remained true to it, probably being granted a little room, or hermit's cell, within the Temple precincts where she could develop her gifts of prophecy and ministry.

The name 'Anna' means 'grace' and grace has been defined as 'an unmerited favour bestowed by God'. Anna's life certainly bears witness to this. Dedicating herself to God, she remains thankful that he accepts her service and allows her to continue. There must have been times when she felt downcast, lonely, frightened, but the thought of the tremendous privilege she enjoyed as a contemplative and bearer of God's word would be sufficient to help her through such crises. Her *perseverance* is eventually rewarded beyond all her expectations. As Mary and Joseph approach to make the customary sacrifice on behalf of their new-born child, Anna has a flash of recognition that this is no ordinary family, no ordinary baby. This is the Chosen One of God, the promised Messiah, sent to redeem Israel and proclaim God's message to the world.

And what does she then do? Luke's Gospel tells us that 'she gave thanks to God; and she talked about the child to all who were looking for the liberation of Jerusalem' (Luke 2:38). In other words, she wants to shout the good news from the roof tops. The coming of Christ into the world is not to be a closely guarded secret shared only by a chosen few. It is an occasion for great rejoicing and is to be communicated to everybody.

In two respects then, Anna can serve as a role model for us all. We are not all called to the contemplative life, but most of us have experienced at one time or another the guidance or blessing of God. We have done nothing to deserve this: we should remember that such insights come to us through the grace of God and that we do not earn them on our own merits. In times of spiritual darkness, however, or when we are tempted to abandon our faith and pursue the easier path of worldly pleasure and diversion, we need to remember the tremendous privilege bestowed upon us during those moments when we did have a vision of God and, like Anna, remain true to this vision. Especially as we grow older we must always recall all the blessings previously experienced and not allow ourselves to succumb to disappointment, bitterness, or feelings of failure. We must persevere and continue our spiritual journey – perhaps through Bible study or renewed church attendance and certainly through private prayer – and then perhaps we, too, will be enabled in some small way to bring the message of Christ to others and thus help in the great task of redemption.

Prayer and reflection

The festival of Candlemas traditionally marks the end of the Christmas and Epiphany seasons in the Church's calendar. In some churches all the candles are blessed on this day and carried round the church in procession, while the

Nunc Dimittis is sung to symbolize the coming of Christ, the True Light, into the temple of our hearts.

> *Lord Jesus Christ, as we light candles at this time of year to remember your Presentation in the Temple, we would present ourselves to you so that, illumined by your Light, we may become living temples of your Spirit and enable others to discover the solace and comfort of your message. Grant us, too, the grace to persevere in our faith so that, day by day, we may come to experience the loving guidance of God more fully and in turn guide others in their journey through the world.*
>
> *We pray, too, for all women who have entered a religious community and taken vows of poverty, chastity, and obedience. We ask, Lord, for your blessing on their work of teaching, healing and service to those in need. We pray that the beauty and order of their disciplined lives may provide inspiration for others, a refuge from the confusion of the world, a place where all may find peace. In this way, Lord, may more and more people be enabled to find you and give thanks for this great blessing which alone can give meaning and purpose to our lives.*

In what ways might we more effectively tell other people about the gospel of Christ?

How can we endeavour to build more moments of contemplation into our lives?

A Sign that will be Spoken Against

It will not be possible
To ignore this child.
Already Simeon and Anna,
Alive to God's ways
Through years of prayer and worship,
Have recognized him.

He is God's sign,
Even to the Gentiles.
He will be hated and reviled,
For he will strip bare
The hidden thoughts and wishes
Of all our hearts.

Luke 2:28–39 RT

Simon's Mother-in-law

Before Lent

On leaving the synagogue he went to Simon's house.
Simon's mother-in-law was in the grip of a high fever;
and they asked him to help her.

(Luke 4:38)

Luke alone of all the Gospel writers recounts for us the story of the boy Jesus, when about twelve years old, staying behind in the Temple at Jerusalem to ask questions of the doctors of the Law. He describes the anxiety of Mary and Joseph when they discover he is missing, their desperate search for him among friends and relatives, their anxious decision to return to Jerusalem, their joy and relief – slightly tinged with anger – when they at last find him safe and sound. How did Luke know these things? We must assume that at some stage of his life he was in close contact with Mary (see Acts 1:14) and that she confided in him not only the secret of her own miraculous conception and visit to Elizabeth, but also what she could remember of Jesus' childhood and how this pointed forward to his later ministry.

Like the other evangelists, Luke then moves on to the

recognition by John the Baptist of Jesus as Messiah and Jesus' subsequent withdrawal into the wilderness. He describes the Temptations – perhaps Our Lord himself told his disciples about this experience – then goes on to record Jesus' return to Nazareth and Capernaum. At Nazareth Jesus visits the synagogue and reads from the Book of the Prophet Isaiah, proclaiming himself as the fulfilment of that prophecy. At Capernaum he teaches the people on the sabbath day and cures a man 'possessed by a demon, an unclean spirit' (Luke 4:33). Luke gives no account of the calling of the first disciples. He assumes that we know who Simon is and takes us straight away into Simon's house where there is someone dangerously ill with a fever.

In the Bible a name is often a clue to the person's charac-ter. We have seen this with Elizabeth and Anna, and in the case of Anna her father's name, Phanuel, which means 'the face of God', is also emphasized, indicating that she was destined to gaze on the Christ-child and see God face to face. We are not, however, given the name of Simon's mother-in-law. We can surmise that she lived with Simon and his wife and had an active role in the household since, as soon as she is healed, 'she got up at once and attended to their needs' (Luke 4:39). Yet, although she has no name, we can learn much about her from this action. She does not rush out to tell the neighbours or throw a party to celebrate her recovery. On the contrary, she immediately thinks about the needs of others and resumes her tasks as a provider of hospitality. In this respect she is a model of Christian service: although not of priestly family and just an ordinary housewife, she puts others first, self last, and is in this way pleasing God.

There is a sense in which, throughout history, women's lives have mirrored the teachings of the Gospels in a very profound way. The nurturing of another human being through the long months of pregnancy, and then through infancy and childhood, and the efficient running of a household, 'making ends meet', are all tasks demanding patience and self-sacrifice. They may not be great or heroic actions in a practical or worldly sense, but they form the rock on which loving and harmonious relationships can be built – they are examples of the way that strives continually for the good of others and does not seek reward. It is interesting to note that Our Lord himself pays tribute to the ordinary household work carried out by women by alluding to it in his parables. 'To what shall I compare the kingdom of God? It is like yeast which a woman took and mixed with three measures of flour till it was all leavened' (Luke 13:20–21). 'Or again, if a woman has ten silver coins and loses one of them, does she not light the lamp, sweep out the house, and look in every corner till she finds it? And when she does, she calls her friends and neighbours together, and says, "Rejoice with me! I have found the coin that I lost" ' (Luke 15:8–9). Simon Peter's mother-in-law must surely have been like this diligent housewife. Perhaps it is not too fanciful to imagine Our Lord watching her as, restored to health, she sets about baking bread for the evening meal, no doubt thanking God for her deliverance and making the ordinary, everyday routine into an act of reverence and praise.

Prayer and reflection

In the interval between Candlemas and Ash Wednesday let us ask for discipline and self-control to go about our daily tasks in a renewed spirit of service, thereby showing our concern for other people. Let us think how we might best restructure our lives so that we have time to pause and give thanks to God, time to listen to the Holy Spirit, time to reflect on our true purpose. So may we be enabled to resist the temptations of the world and live our lives for the benefit of others to God's praise and glory.

Let us pray, too, for all organizations of Christian women which strive to uphold family life and values. May we never despise, nor take for granted, the effort which goes into creating a loving home. Let us remember all who struggle against the odds in difficult financial circumstances, and pray that those who are better off may be kind, compassionate and generous. In this way may homes throughout our land reflect the warmth of Christian love and be the foundation stones of God's Kingdom here on earth.

Do we nowadays sufficiently value the roles of wife and mother?

How can we help to promote harmonious family life as a Christian ideal?

Women of the Passion

Lent, Passiontide and Easter

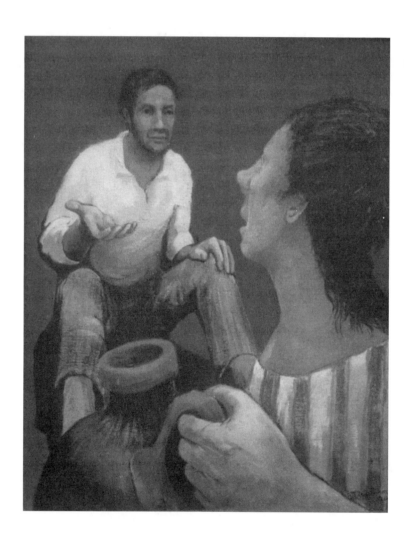

The Woman of Samaria

Ash Wednesday

It was about noon, and Jesus, tired after his journey, was sitting by the well. His disciples had gone into town to buy food. Meanwhile *a Samaritan woman came to draw water*, and Jesus said to her, 'Give me a drink.'

(John 4:6–8)

Ash Wednesday, the start of Lent, is a solemn occasion when many churches hold special services. John's Gospel is a solemn and mysterious Gospel, differing from the other three in its chronology and containing many incidents not otherwise mentioned. This story of Jesus' encounter with a woman of Samaria is not recorded elsewhere and relates to the beginning of his adult ministry when both he and John the Baptist were baptizing in Judaea.

It seems that Jesus, anxious not to be seen as competing with John, decides to return to Galilee, choosing a route through Samaria, a region usually shunned by devout Jews since, because of an ancient quarrel, they consider the Samaritans an unclean and godless people. Jesus himself has no such scruples. He sends the disciples into a nearby town to buy food, and when a Samaritan woman approaches the well where he is resting he asks her to draw water for him so that he can have a refreshing drink. These actions alone have great significance: they show that Jesus experienced moments of hunger, fatigue and thirst just as we all do, but – although sharing in our human nature – he rises above our petty squabbles and prejudices and extends his mission of love and redemption to everyone, regardless of race, class or gender.

The woman herself is startled to be addressed in this way by a Jewish stranger. 'What! You, a Jew, ask for a drink from a Samaritan woman?' (v. 9). But she is even more amazed, and possibly also a little frightened, when he begins to reveal to her that he knows all her secrets, including the fact that she has had five husbands and that 'the man you are living with now is not your husband' (v. 18). The woman is, in other words, someone of very dubious reputation, notorious within her community and certainly not a person with whom strictly religious people would wish to be associated. But here again Jesus shows us that the wisdom of God is very different from the wisdom of men and, as we read in the Old Testament, 'the Lord does not see as a mortal sees; mortals see only appearances but the Lord sees into the heart' (1 Samuel 16:7).

There is something rather remarkable about this woman. First of all, she comes to the well alone and not in the company and protection of other women. Then, when asked to draw water, she does not turn back out of modesty and fear at having been approached by a stranger, nor does she instantly obey. Instead, she questions the stranger's behaviour in speaking to her and then engages in a dialogue with him, at first scornful of his claim that he can provide 'living water' but, as the conversation proceeds, aware that he has some extraordinary power which forces her into reverence. Even so, when asked to fetch her husband, she does not bow her head in shame, but boldly proclaims her unmarried status. She seems proud of it, defiant of convention. Then, when Jesus reveals that he knows about her current relationship, she makes no apology, but shows a high degree of intelligence and discernment. 'Sir, I can see you are a prophet' (v. 19).

What are we to make of all this? Have we misjudged her? It is possible that she has been *widowed* five times (this might easily happen in the dangerous circumstances of first-century Palestine), but it could also be that her strong and intelligent personality was not content to be entirely submissive to a husband's authority and that she has been divorced or 'put aside' five times for disobedience. In the Sermon on the Mount Christ alludes to such practices when he reminds his hearers (Matthew 5:31–32) that the only real cause for divorce should be unchastity, and William Barclay in his commentary on *The Gospel of Matthew* explains that one school of Jewish thought interpreted the Law of Moses (Deuteronomy 24:1) in the widest possible manner:

> They said that it meant that a man could divorce his wife if she spoiled his dinner by putting too much salt in his food, if she went in public with her head uncovered, if she talked with men in the streets, if she was a brawling woman, if she spoke disrespectfully

of her husband's parents in his presence, if she was troublesome or quarrelsome. (vol. 1, p. 150)

Looked at from this angle, this Samaritan woman is perhaps not the immoral adulteress she is often made out to be, but someone not afraid to champion women's rights and, as such, accorded here a dignity and value by Our Lord. Women are not to be treated as mere goods and chattels, to be disposed of at will or on a whim. Nor are they to be reviled when they rebel against such degradation. It is noteworthy that the woman commands some kind of authority in her local community. When she goes back into the town people listen to what she has to say, and many of them become believers (vv. 39–42).

Some versions of John's Gospel also include the story of the woman taken in the act of adultery (generally placed at John 8:1–11 although this is often disputed). It is easy to see why this passage is so controversial. The woman *is* guilty, but Jesus does not condemn her. He admonishes her and tells her to leave her life of sin. This does not mean that he condones her unchastity, but what he really wishes to expose is the hypocrisy of the Pharisees. 'If anyone is without sin among you, let him be the first to throw a stone at her.' It is a rebuke which reminds us that none of us is perfect, that we all have our faults and should not sit in judgement upon others too hastily. The beginning of Lent is a time when we should therefore search our consciences, ask ourselves serious questions about our own conduct, and tighten up our spiritual discipline.

Prayer and reflection

Dear Lord, as we now start this solemn season of Lent, help us to recognize our own faults and failings before we have the presumption to judge others. Help us, too, to be merciful to those who have fallen into sinful ways, remembering that in your sight they are not beyond redemption and praying that, by your grace, we may find how best to counsel and correct them. We ask this, Lord, in your name.

Can we be too liberal in our treatment of offenders?

How, as Christians, can we best minister to those in prison and those convicted of serious crimes?

The Samaritan Woman

He was a perfect stranger –
But that's never bothered me,
I'll talk to anyone, and besides,
Not too many in the village
Have much time for me these days.

I was a bit surprised
When he made the first approach,
Asking help from me, a Samaritan,
And a woman at that.
But I got him his drink.

I couldn't understand
When he said I should have asked him
For some special water
That would quench your thirst for ever:
I thought I'd like to try that!

He told me to fetch my husband.
Well, I wasn't going into details for him,
So I said I hadn't one.
But he got straight to the truth –
It seems he knew all about me.

It was just too close for comfort,
So I tried a bit of religious diversion.
He was clearly a Jew,
So the old chestnut about their Temple
Versus our Holy Mountain seemed a good one.
But he was having none of that.

Then this perfect stranger
Told me who he was.
I had to believe him, though I couldn't think why
He had bothered with me.
And nor could his friends.

I ran back to the village
And shouted my news.
That got them talking:
Me, wanting to share this man with them
Was stretching belief!

Listen, my friend,
They had to meet him for themselves
Before they understood what I was saying.
So come – see this man, who told me
All things that I ever did.

John 4:5–30 RT

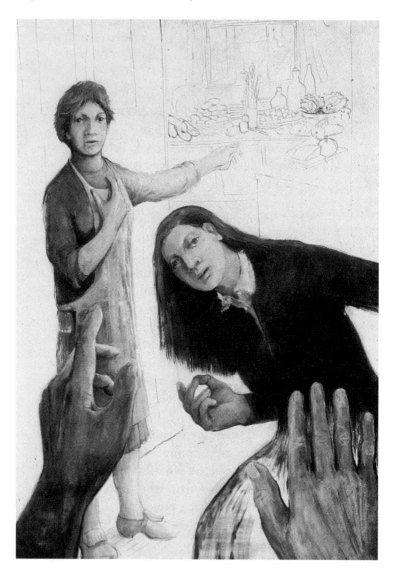

Martha

Lent 1

Six days before the Passover festival Jesus came to
Bethany, the home of Lazarus whom he had raised
from the dead. They gave a supper in his honour, *at
which Martha served.*

(John 12:1–2)

Palm Sunday often falls in early April. It is a changeable
season, both in Britain and in Israel. In either country it
can be cold, damp and wet, or gloriously sunny and warm.
One particular year I awoke to a brilliantly clear morning,
the birds were singing and it seemed as if Spring had come.
As I walked to church along a quiet lane I noticed the
celandines in the hedgerows, glinting gold against a background of green. Young rabbits were frolicking across the
fields, and everywhere there were signs of new life and
hope.

This was important for me, as I had just suffered
bereavement, and I was reminded that in John's Gospel
the Passion narrative is preceded by the account of the
raising of Lazarus at Bethany. Matthew, Mark and Luke

all agree with John that at the start of what we now call Holy Week Jesus was at Bethany, just a mile or two from Jerusalem, and the tradition is that the triumphal entry into the Holy City, at which the crowds scattered palms at his feet, took place from there. Bethany was the home village of the two sisters, Martha and Mary, and it is thus appropriate that we should begin our Lenten meditations with Martha.

What else do we know about her? Luke's Gospel portrays her in a different light. We are told that, while Jesus and the disciples were on their way to Jerusalem, they 'came to a village where a woman named Martha made him welcome' (Luke 10:38). Martha goes to prepare a meal, while her sister Mary sits at Jesus' feet, listening to his teaching. Martha, Luke continues, 'was distracted by her many tasks' and complains bitterly that Mary is not helping her. 'Lord, do you not care that my sister has left me to get on with the work by myself? Tell her to come and give me a hand.' She is then apparently rebuked by Our Lord who says, 'Martha, Martha, you are fretting and fussing about so many things; only one thing is necessary.'

This story has traditionally given Martha a bad reputation. She is generally presented to us as the busy, house-proud woman who turns every occasion into a nightmare for both herself and her guests, by her anxiety and perfectionism. She is so concerned to make a good impression and to display her culinary skills that she overlooks the most important thing of all, the fact that Jesus is in her house and has chosen her home as a place to expound his gospel of love.

William Barclay, in his *Commentary on the Gospel of*

Luke, sees Martha as an example of misplaced kindness. Jesus, says Barclay, had come to Bethany 'to find an oasis of calm away from the demanding crowds', to experience some peace and tranquillity, and all Martha can do is upset the whole household and insist on the best possible meal with no doubt the best cutlery and the best dinner-service, in the belief that this is what hospitality demands. So Martha, according to Barclay, is 'really being unkind to him whose heart cried for quiet'. However, this is not the only view. The great German medieval mystic, Eckhart, who lived between 1260 and 1328, actually places Martha on a higher spiritual level than Mary. 'Every good thing,' he writes, 'both temporal and eternal, that a creature could possess was fully possessed by Martha.' Christ's address to her, 'Martha, Martha,' was not a rebuke that she was in the wrong and Mary in the right, but merely a reassurance, he believes, that Mary, too, is learning to be as Martha and one day will succeed in being so.

At first sight this looks like sheer perversity, and yet there is a strong medieval tradition that depicts Martha as a dragon-slayer, a conqueror. In some medieval paintings she is portrayed as a mature, powerful woman who, with a cross and sprinkler of holy water in one hand, has subdued a snake-like monster, which she has bound with her girdle and which now lies tamed and defeated at her feet. This is the Martha of the Johannine story, the Martha who refuses to accept the finality of death, the Martha who goes out to meet Jesus while Mary stays at home, the Martha who boldly proclaims, 'Lord, if you had been here my brother would not have died. Even now I know that God will grant you whatever you ask of him' (John

11:21–22). Perhaps, therefore, we should examine this story in a little more detail.

When Martha hears that Jesus is coming she goes out straight away to meet him. Perhaps even now there is something to be done, perhaps even now death can be reversed by this strange man whom everyone acknowledges as a teacher and prophet. Have there not been reports of such occurrences? Perhaps Martha is thinking of the widow of Nain, whose son was restored to life, or of Jairus's daughter who was also given up for dead, but then made a miraculous recovery? There must have been witnesses to these events, and rumours about them must have been current. Jesus does not at first promise anything spectacular. He reminds Martha that there is a Jewish belief that the dead will rise again for a final judgement at the end of time. Then, when Martha gives him an affirmation of this belief, he makes the dramatic statement that he himself is the Resurrection and the Life, and suddenly Martha realizes what is really happening. This Galilean, whom they have welcomed into their house and whom they regard as a wise and special friend, is not just a great prophet in the tradition of Elijah or John the Baptist, but, as Martha now says, 'the Messiah, the Son of God who was to come into the world'.

Several commentators have pointed out that Martha's proclamation at this point is very akin to Peter's on witnessing the Transfiguration. Indeed, Martha and Peter have much in common. Both come across as strong, outspoken personalities. Both have their moments of weakness and backsliding. Martha, for instance, despite her confession of faith, is reluctant to see the tomb opened when Jesus

gives the order to do so. Yet this must not divert us from
the fact that it is Martha whose act of faith calls forth from
Jesus one of the greatest statements of the New Testament,
those words which have brought comfort to so many, the
expression of the Christian hope for all believers. 'Jesus
said, "I am the resurrection and the life. Whoever has faith
in me shall live, even though he dies; and no one who lives
and has faith in me shall ever die"' (John 11:25–26).

Which then is the true Martha? Martha, the busy, bust-
ling housewife, traditionally regarded as the patron saint
of housekeepers? Or Martha, the determined matron, a
female St George, who overcomes the dragon of death,
refusing to be defeated by it? Perhaps both images are true.
Why not? Down-to-earth practical people often have great
spiritual insights. My great-grandmother, appropriately
enough, was called Martha. There is a story about her
that once, when there was an outbreak of smallpox in the
isolated farming community where she lived, she insisted
on cooking and baking food for the victims. She would
leave it on their doorsteps and collect the pans and dishes
later. When someone warned her that even so she could
still catch the infection, she is said to have replied that it
was a Christian duty to tend the sick and she believed God
would protect her. She remained unscathed, and all the
victims recovered. I like to think that Our Lord would
have said of her, 'Truly, your faith has saved you.'

Mark's Gospel tells us that the meal at Bethany took
place in the house of Simon the leper, and many commentators have detected some confused memories here, since
Martha, they say, would surely not serve at table in someone else's house. But why not? A leper in those days would

be ostracized, an outcast, a person shunned by others out of fear of contamination. Jesus, we know, made a special point of seeking out such people, and it is highly probable that Simon of Bethany, knowing this, invited him into his household. But who would do the cooking? Once again, Martha comes to the rescue. Just as she overcomes her misgivings and gives the signal to unseal the tomb – and we must remember that for the Jews, to touch or even to see a dead body meant defilement – so too she has sufficient faith to help Simon entertain Our Lord. It must have seemed a strange thing to do, but Martha was an extraordinary woman. She did not care what the neighbours thought. She saw what needed to be done, went ahead, and did it.

'They gave a supper in his honour *at which Martha served*.' Nothing in John's Gospel is superfluous, and this phrase is highly significant. John, too, recounts the episode when Christ himself washes the disciples' feet and describes himself as a servant. 'I have set you an example; you are to do as I have done for you.' Martha certainly fulfils this requirement. There she is, a strong, practical, energetic person, perhaps the eldest of the household, used to running her own home and to being in charge of things, but able at the same time to humble herself and minister to the needs of others. Seen from this angle, Eckhart's words are not so puzzling. Martha does not need to be *shown* how to live a Christian life; she *is* a Christian already, by instinct, by nature, and as such is to be an example to us all. All of us are called upon in some way to serve others, and in so doing perhaps we too will find that spiritual strength that is able to look death and disaster squarely in the face and so help life to continue.

Prayer and reflection

Read the relevant passages:
  John 11:1–44 and 12:1–2.
  Luke 10:38–42.
Is Barclay right? Can one be too fussy? Or is Eckhart nearer the truth? How can we better appreciate Martha's spirituality?

Martha's words at John 11:24 are an echo of Job 19:25, so memorably set to music by Handel in his *Messiah*. Perhaps find an opportunity to listen to this piece of music (the aria 'I know that my Redeemer liveth') and meditate upon it.

Martha's faith was strong, even in her deep bereavement. So often bereavement is a time when so many lose faith, especially if they have had to see a loved one suffer, or when death has come unexpectedly or in tragic circumstances. Let us remember all such people in our prayers and ask that they may be helped and comforted.

Dear Lord Jesus, who comforted Martha on the loss of her brother Lazarus and reassured her that the dear departed will rise again, comfort and heal, we beseech you, all those who even now are weighed down by the traumas of grief. Be near to them in their sadness that they may feel supported by your presence; help them to trust in you as one who can lift them out of despondency and despair; and guide them towards a deeper faith in you as the source of everlasting life. We ask this, Lord, in your dear Name.

Martha in the House of Simon the Leper

If my Lord can go there,
So can I

If my Lord can eat there,
So can I

If my Lord can speak to him,
So can I

If my Lord can heal him ...
... ...
This I do not dare

I only dare to lend a helping hand
And cook for him
And wait on him at table.

How can *we* make our lives more truly devoted to the
service of others?

Martha

What was Martha feeling,
Scurrying around so busily
To serve the essential needs
Of her guests?
Did she resent not being able
To join the company?
Could she have done less –
Prepared a simpler meal,
Or left the pots and pans until morning?
Or was there some guilt – some feeling of inferiority –
That she actually did not enjoy the cut and thrust
Of theological debate,
And was happier in her kitchen?

Mary

And what was Mary doing,
Escaping the traditional woman's role,
Usurping that favoured position at the Rabbi's feet,
Listening and learning with the men?
She had decided, with admirable strength of purpose,
That this was important to her –
But did she also have a sneaking suspicion
That Martha's complaint
Was absolutely justified?

The Lord

Martha's relationship with the Master was robust.
She did not wait to consider her words,
And he was equally direct:
He would not criticize the choice that Mary made,
However unfeminine – or feminist! – this seemed to be.
But this empowering ability to choose
Was available to Martha too,
That she might return to her strengths
Uncluttered with resentment or choking envy:
Her preferred way as honoured and as valid
As her sister's.

Luke 10:38–42 RT

Mary at Bethany

Lent 2

Then Mary brought a pound of very costly perfume,
pure oil of nard, and anointed Jesus's feet and wiped
them with her hair, till the house was filled with the
fragrance.

(John 12:3)

April, as the poet T. S. Eliot once reminded us, can be a
cruel month. There are mild Spring days, when the new
flowers venture forth, but then there can be bitterly cold
winds which destroy the daffodils, and blow the early blos-
som off the trees. 'What a shame!' I heard someone say as
she contemplated my garden after a sudden hailstorm.
'What a waste!' And yet the flowers *had* been there, and
I was able to salvage some of them and put them in a vase
within the house.

Are good things ever wasted? That is the question that
confronts us as we consider the continuation in John's
Gospel of the story of the Feast at Bethany. Imagine the
scene. It is a strange event by any standards. John does
not contradict Mark's earlier account that Jesus and the

disciples are in the house of Simon the leper. If this is indeed the case, what an occasion it must have been for Simon! Shunned, feared because of the nature of his illness, perhaps disfigured and misshapen, he suddenly finds himself surrounded by people, led by the indomitable Martha, and his house is filled with love, laughter and rejoicing. Then another woman comes, obviously very excited, bent on doing something very unusual. She rushes into the room where the feast is being held – the guests, by the way, according to Palestinian custom, are probably sitting in a big circle in the largest room while the food is brought to them from the kitchen – and, going up to Jesus, pours a whole box of very expensive ointment over his feet. It seems she has acted on impulse, for she has forgotten to bring with her any towel or cloth, and she has used too much ointment and it is very sticky. So, again, on impulse and regardless of the fact that it was considered scandalous for a woman to uncover her head in public, she removes her head covering, unbinds her hair, and throws herself down at Jesus' feet, by now perhaps almost hysterical, beside herself with emotion. No wonder the disciples and other people present are shocked and taken aback. Not only has this woman behaved in a very startling and improper way, throwing herself at the Master in a very wanton manner, but she has also been very extravagant and wasteful. Judas voices their disapproval. What a pity the seal has been broken! What a shame the ointment is running all over the place! How much better it would have been if the woman had restrained herself and perhaps asked *him* first what she should do in the Master's honour. He, Judas, would have been able to advise her.

Mark's Gospel recounts the same incident but does not actually name the woman. John is adamant (John 11:2) that it *is* Mary, the sister of Martha and Lazarus. There is something puzzling about this. Can it be that Mary's behaviour on this occasion was so uncharacteristic that people afterwards simply couldn't believe it of her? (There is a tradition that identifies Mary of Bethany with Mary of Magdala, who is held to be a reformed prostitute, but there is no real scriptural authority for either assumption.) We know from other accounts that Mary was of a quiet, even timid, nature. John tells us that, after the death of Lazarus, 'as soon as Martha heard that Jesus was on his way, she went to meet him, and left Mary sitting at home' (John 11:20). Martha is the impulsive one here; Mary, overcome with grief, seems to lack the will-power even to go out to welcome the man she has previously acknowledged as a great teacher and healer. Luke's Gospel gives the famous portrayal of Mary sitting at Jesus' feet, listening to his words and forgetting about the housework. She seems here to be a contemplative, and not a particularly active person, perhaps even inclined to depression and inertia.

It is interesting to look again at Eckhart's commentary. 'Mary', he says, 'was filled with longing, longing she knew not why and wanting she knew not what. We suspect that she, dear Mary, sat there a little more for her own happiness than for spiritual profit.' That is why, according to Eckhart, Martha rebukes her and asks Our Lord to do the same. Mary, says Eckhart, has not yet acquired that selfless spirit of service that characterizes Martha and that alone can triumph over all adversity and disappointment. 'When Mary sat at the feet of Our Lord', he continues, 'she was

learning, for she had just gone to school to learn how
to live.' Jesus recognizes this and allows her to stay, an
unheard-of privilege for a woman in those times, since
women were not generally permitted to listen to the rabbis
in this way, not even in the synagogues. On the later
occasion, as he approaches the tomb of her brother, Jesus
sends for her. 'The Master is here', says Martha, 'and is
asking for you' (John 11:28). It is this message that stirs
Mary from her lethargy and once again enables her to act.
She goes out to meet Jesus, and it is the sight of Mary,
with tears streaming down her face and overcome
with grief, that finally moves him to show the greatest
compassion of which God is capable and restore Lazarus
to life. 'When Jesus saw her weeping and the Jews who
had come with her weeping, he was moved with
indignation and deeply distressed. "Where have you laid
him?" he asked. They replied, "Come and see"' (John
11:33–34).

Is this why she dashes in at the feast with her box of
ointment and breaks it open in such a dramatic way? Jesus
answers the angry criticism of the other guests by saying
'She has anointed my body in anticipation of my burial'
(Mark 14:8). But can Mary really have known this? Is it
not more likely that *her* motivation was different? That
she acts out of gratitude and sheer joy because her brother
has been restored to her and she herself has come back
to life? Barclay's commentary suggests that Mary's action
shows the extravagance of love. 'Mary took the most precious thing she possessed and spent it all on Jesus. Love is
not love if it nicely calculates the cost.' Furthermore, he
says, Mary here shows her great humility. 'It was a sign

of honour to anoint a person's head . . . But Mary would not look so high as the head of Jesus; she anointed his feet. The last thing that Mary thought of was to confer an honour upon Jesus. She never dreamed she was good enough for that.'

Yet we must, of course, take Our Lord's comment into consideration. He replies to Mary's generous gift with his own generosity of spirit. He does not chastise her. The box of ointment could certainly have been sold and the money given to the poor, but that was not what Mary wanted. She wanted to do something *for Jesus*, and he uses the opportunity to warn his disciples of what is about to happen. No good thing is ever wasted; no good intention is ever lost in the sight of God. The whole house, according to John, was filled with the fragrance. Mary's deed was so beautiful that everyone who approached it in the right spirit could derive benefit from it.

My mother passed the last week of her life in a hospice. One day a friend came in with some very expensive perfume. Mother smiled and said, 'You shouldn't have spent all that money on me.' But she asked me to open the bottle and put a few drops on her hands and wrists and then, after her death, to give the rest to another patient.

Prayer and reflection

Read the relevant passages:
John 12:1–8.
Mark 14:1–11.
What differences can be noted between the two accounts?

What insights can be gained from a study of these differences?

Note the comments about Judas Iscariot. Here, too, are several further points for consideration. What is it that Judas really finds so shocking? Why is this perhaps the final thing that makes him decide to betray his Master?

Re-read Mark 14:1–11 and try to imagine the scene. Perhaps even *try to act it* and see if further light can be shed on Mary's action. Then read Luke 10:38–42 and John 11:17–37. What picture do we gain of Mary from these passages? Could it be that she was suffering from depression? (Note that neither Martha nor Mary appears to have a husband. Could it be that they were widows? Or had they remained unmarried, possibly because they were poor and had no dowry?)

Mary was perhaps not as strong a character as Martha. She seems to have been quiet and reserved, easily upset and also deeply emotional. Yet this is her way of seeking the love of God and, once she has found it, she seeks to share her joy with others. She looked for grace and was rewarded with a gladness of heart; she appealed to the goodness of God and responded to this with her own generosity of spirit. So let us pray that we, too, may be generous and joyful in our response to Our Lord's infinite kindness and compassion:

> *Dear Lord and Saviour, teach us through the example of Mary of Bethany to listen to your words and seek to understand them ever more deeply. Teach us to be*

ever more mindful of your mercy and grace towards us and your healing power. So may we, too, Lord, come to be generous in spirit, giving thanks for all our many blessings and constantly seeking to share our joy with others. Prevent us from being mean and selfish with our gifts and our possessions, and enable us to see how we can best employ them in your service. We ask this in your name.

Mary of Bethany in the House of Simon the Leper

I *will* break through:
You shall not stop me.

I *will* break the seals:
You shall not restrain me.

I *will* pour my oil over his tired feet:
You, Simon, did not even offer water.

You stand aghast
No-one comes to help me
No-one brings a cloth or towel.

No matter. I have my hair,
A gift of God, whatever you may say about it.
And I'll use my gifts
To help my Master.

He will not despise me.

How can *we* be more generous in our giving?

Rhoda

Lent 3

So the other disciple, the high priest's acquaintance, went back and spoke to *the girl on duty at the door*, and brought Peter in. The girl said to Peter, 'Are you another of this man's disciples?' 'I am not,' he said.

(John 18:16–17)

Much has happened between the Feast at Bethany in the house of Simon, the leper, and the incident recounted above in the courtyard of the High Priest's house. Jesus, it seems, has journeyed daily into Jerusalem and taught there in the Temple. On one occasion he 'drove out all who were buying and selling in the temple precincts' and the crowds 'went wild with excitement' (Matthew 21:12, 10). The next day, according to Matthew, 'on his way to the city, he felt hungry; and seeing a fig tree at the roadside he went up to it, but found nothing on it but leaves. He said to the tree, "May you never bear fruit again!" and at once the tree withered away' (Matthew 21:18–19). Later that same week he gave his disciples instructions as regards the preparation of the Passover; they met in the Upper Room and

witnessed the institution of the Holy Sacrament. Afterwards they all went out to the Mount of Olives and
watched in fear and trembling as Jesus prayed in anguish
in the Garden of Gethesemane. Then the soldiers burst in
upon them, led by the traitor, Judas. Jesus is arrested and
taken off to stand trial before the High Priest on a charge
of blasphemy, which would be punishable by death. The
events of Holy Week are so fast-moving and dramatic,
there is so much that is puzzling and disturbing that most
commentators overlook the girl on duty at the door, the
next female figure to appear in the Passion narratives.

Yet all four Gospels mention her. The accounts vary
slightly, but all agree that Peter's first denial was provoked
by her accusation, and John adds the significant detail that
she was a portress, perhaps a kind of *concièrge*. John also
relates that the mysterious other disciple, thought by many
to be John himself, actually speaks to her, presumably
asking for Peter to be admitted. Does this imply that at
least one of the disciples already knew her quite well?
Dorothy L. Sayers in her dramatization of the Gospel narratives, *The Man Born to be King*, certainly thinks so. In
the tenth play of her series, entitled *The Princes of this
World*, she imagines John as having some connection with
the High Priest's house and thus being able to gain access.
The portress herself seems to be a decent, good-hearted
girl, ready to exchange back-chat with the guards or do a
good turn to a friend, without much thought one way or
the other. In Sayers' view, she is not nasty or malicious,
merely curious as to what is going on and what all the
excitement is about. In this play she is given the name of
Tabitha, which means 'a gazelle'.

Abraham Kuyper in his classic study *Women of the New Testament* has a different interpretation. He sees this girl and the other maidservant mentioned in some accounts as afflicted by 'the sin of vanity, the vanity of gossipy women'. 'Such vanity', he says, 'squelched the better urges of their hearts, smothered any sympathy they might have had for a friend of the prisoner, and enabled them to take delight in seeing the deadly fear which crept over Peter's features' (p. 66). In their desire to draw attention to themselves and to gain merit in the eyes of their employers they deliberately cause embarrassment to Peter, trying to denounce him. Their teasing of Peter is wicked, their gossiping with the bystanders has an evil intention, they themselves are complacent and self-satisfied. It is a very strong condemnation.

Now we all know that there are indeed such people. In Nazi Germany, in Stalinist Russia, at the time of the Inquisition and the witchcraft trials, there were those who sought to ingratiate themselves with the authorities by spying on others, passing on information about them, and acting as *agents provocateurs*. But was this maidservant really like this? It could be significant that the word actually used in both Mark and Luke is *paidiske*, a little maid, perhaps a mere child. In this case her question to Peter could have been one of sheer innocence, without any secondary motivation.

Whatever she was – flirtatious girl, spiteful older woman, or very young child – this person was certainly a servant, and it is worth considering other references to servants in the Bible or stories about them. From Old Testament documents, where the word translated as 'maid' is frequently *amah*, a hand-maid, we know that such people were little more than slaves, regarded as the property of their masters or mistresses, and frequently abused by them. (See Genesis 16, the story of Hagar, or Exodus 21, where we have a kind of servants' charter designed to curb some of the worst excesses.) On the other hand, in the Second Book of Kings we hear about a captive who, no doubt because she was well treated, is instrumental in curing her mistress's husband of leprosy (2 Kings 5:1–5). This little girl, by telling her foreign captors about the prophet Elisha, becomes a channel of redemption.

There is a legend – admittedly without much scriptural foundation – that identifies the maid on duty in the High Priest's house with the Rhoda who is mentioned in Acts 12:13. This girl is also a doorkeeper, but the house is now that of Mary, mother of John Mark, where the disciples have sought shelter after the imprisonment of Peter. Rhoda recognizes Peter's voice, even while he is still outside, and is so overjoyed that he has found them again that she quite forgets, in her excitement, to let him in and leaves him standing in the street while she hurries away to tell the household. One can see how the legend arises. Stricken by remorse over her denunciation of Peter, the High Priest's maidservant has now herself joined the small band of Jesus' followers and found a new position with a Christian employer. Far-fetched? Perhaps. But it is nevertheless tempting to believe that, like Peter himself, this girl had a change of heart. Perhaps she, too, saw Jesus being led out into the courtyard. Perhaps he also looked at her and in his gaze she saw not only a profound sorrow over what she had done, but also a profound forgiveness. The gospel of Christ teaches that no one is beyond redemption. Peter is given another chance. Perhaps the maid, too, is given the grace to change her whole life and thus become an example and inspiration to others.

Prayer and reflection

Read the accounts in all four Gospels. What other clues are there as to the maidservant's character and behaviour?

Most commentators think that the other disciple 'known to the High Priest' must have been John, but some think it might have been Judas. What difference would this make to our interpretation of the maid's denunciation and Peter's denial?

Is it true that no one is beyond redemption? Even Judas?

Look up other references to maids and maidservants in a concordance. Perhaps consider what light is thrown by such passages on Luke 1:38.

Read the story in Acts 12. Then try to imagine the incident in the High Priest's courtyard and the incident recounted in Acts 12 in the house in Jerusalem. What might Rhoda have said when she rushed back with the news of Peter's miraculous release?

If a copy can be obtained from a local library, a play-reading of *The Princes of this World* might also provoke further thought about this aspect of the Passion.

The girl on duty at the door might have been genuinely

curious as to what was going on in the middle of the night
with such obvious agitation and urgency. Her question to
Peter could just possibly have been inspired by a desire to
learn more about Jesus of Nazareth and his teaching. Or
it could have arisen from a malicious intention to provoke
and denounce and itself have been based on hearsay and
gossip about this band of strange people from Galilee who
seemed to be causing so much disturbance in the Holy
City. And when does curiosity to find out more about
people degenerate into gossip that can hurt and harm? We
need to pray for guidance in this respect and guidance in
our speech and thoughts.

Dear Lord and Father of Mankind, forgive our fool-
ish ways. Help us always to speak with tact and sensi-
tivity so that we do not embarrass, hurt or wound
other people. Guide our speech in such a way that
people may always hear the voice of genuine concern
and compassion. Help us to be good listeners. Above
all, gracious Lord, help us to resist the temptation to
gossip and to spread rumour and scandal. Save us
from hasty judgements and from the desire to con-
demn or plot the downfall of others. When we our-
selves are the victims of calumny, teasing, or malice,
help us to bear such assaults with patience and not
react with anger or bitterness or allow ourselves to
be provoked into actions we shall later regret. In this
way, Lord, may we be given grace to remain true to
your purposes and fulfil our calling as your disciples.
Through Jesus Christ, Our Lord.

In the Portress's Lodge. At Night

I really only meant to tease him.
It was that funny Northern accent –
Those flat vowels and that rough, gruff voice.
You could tell at once he wasn't one of us.
And as I'd heard about that man from Galilee
– Though, come to think of it, no one ever said
He was a country yokel, they all said
He had authority –
I just thought it would be fun to see
How the stranger might react.
I was not prepared for the violence of his answer.
He almost struck me.
Indeed, I'm sure he would have done,
Had not our lads been there from the Guard.
I was very frightened.
That's why I challenged him again.
I had to prove my point and show
That we here in Jerusalem do have some status and
    sophistication.
Then *He* came out and looked at him –
I do not know what happened there.
I only know *He* also looked at me.

Have *we* ever been guilty of teasing or malicious gossip?
If so, how can we make amends?

Claudia

Lent 4

While Pilate was sitting in court *a message came to him from his wife:* 'Have nothing to do with that innocent man; I was much troubled on his account in my dreams last night.'

(Matthew 27:19)

Charged by the Sanhedrin with blasphemy, Christ is now brought before the Roman governor, Pontius Pilate. We have to remember that Palestine was under Roman occupation at the time, and for this reason it was necessary to have the consent of the governor if the death sentence was to be carried out. Pilate is at first very reluctant to agree to the Sanhedrin's demands. Matthew tells us that 'he knew it was out of malice that Jesus had been handed over to him' (Matthew 27:18) and it is at this point that he receives a message from his wife warning him not to proceed with the condemnation.

Matthew's Gospel is the only one to record this incident. How did the writer know about it? Obviously the servant or slave who brought the message must have told other people, and many rumours must have circulated. The message is important because according to Dorothy L. Sayers, it is 'the reagent which crystallizes [Pilate's] vague distrust and antagonism'. Pilate decides to re-try the case, and the Sanhedrin are thus forced, as Matthew tells us, to stir up the crowd to demand crucifixion. This does not exonerate Pilate. Indeed, he *knows* that Jesus is innocent, but he does at least make an attempt to find a way out by declaring that, in Roman law, no crime has been committed.

In the scene in her play *The Princes of this World* where Pilate receives the message, Dorothy L. Sayers imagines that the words have been written on a wax tablet – as would have been the Roman practice in those days – and that they had been 'scored with such urgency' that the stylus had gone clean through the wax. 'Have nothing to do with him,' Pilate repeats. 'What am I to make of that?' What are we to make of it? What kind of woman was Pilate's wife? What kind of dream was it that so impelled her to try to influence her husband's decision?

According to the traditions of the Eastern Church, the descendant of the earliest Christian communities where such things would have been known and talked about, her name was Claudia Procula and she herself later became a Christian martyr. Abraham Kuyper in his book says that we should not speculate about her dream but many, including Dorothy L. Sayers, have done so. In the next play of her cycle, *King of Sorrows*, which depicts the crucifixion, she makes Claudia give an account of her dream as follows: she tells Pilate that she was in a ship at sea, cruising among the calm waters of the Greek islands. Then, suddenly, a storm blew up, the sky darkened, and out of the East came a terrible cry:

Pan ho megas tethnéke! Pan ho megas technéke! She asks
the captain what it means and he replies that it is Greek for
'Great Pan is dead!' 'But how can God die?' she queries, and
the captain then says – and this is the real horror for Claudia
– 'Don't you remember? They crucified Him. He suffered
under Pontius Pilate.' She then hears all the other people in
the ship chanting in various languages: '*He suffered under
Pontius Pilate.*' '*Sub Pontio Pilato crucifixus est.*' '*Gekreu-
zigt unter Pontius Pilatus,*' and so forth. These are, of course,
the words of the Christian creeds which fix the intervention
of God as Saviour at a definite point in history.

At least one other writer, almost an exact contemporary
of Dorothy L. Sayers, has a very similar vision. Gertrud
von le Fort (1876–1971) was the daughter of a Prussian
nobleman of Huguenot descent. One of the first women
in Germany to be allowed to study theology at university,
she was received into the Roman Catholic church in 1926
and subsequently made her name as a poet and novelist of
deep spiritual conviction. Her novella *Die Frau des Pilatus*
(*The Wife of Pilate*) was first published in 1955 and, since
it is not easily accessible in English, it is perhaps allowable
to give a short summary of it here. The narrative takes the
form of a letter written by one of Claudia's Greek servants
to a Christian convert. In it she tells how the events of that
fateful night in Jerusalem altered the course of Claudia's
whole life. Claudia is portrayed here as a young bride,
deeply attached to her much older husband who, according
to Gertrud von le Fort, is the only person involved in the
trial of Christ to have had any inkling of the momentous
nature of the events taking place. The setting of the dream
is slightly different – Claudia imagines herself in a series

of strange buildings, which the reader instantly recognizes as Christian churches – but the terrifying aspect is the same. It is as if Claudia is being given an insight into centuries still to come, and everywhere, at all times and in all places, she hears the words repeated in different languages: *Crucifixus etiam pro nobis sub Pontio Pilato*. She cannot understand what is happening, and then, as she recounts the dream to her servant, they hear the cry of the crowd outside: 'Crucify him! Crucify him!' They watch from a balcony as Pilate desperately tries to prevent a riot, and what strikes them overwhelmingly about the prisoner is the look of infinite compassion on his face as he encounters his accusers. This more than anything else convinces Claudia that her husband is about to commit a very grave injustice which will haunt them for the rest of their lives. She tries to prevent this by sending him a message about the dream, but he shrugs it aside, and afterwards refuses to discuss the incident any further. Claudia and Pilate return to Rome, but Claudia is profoundly changed. Whereas Pilate represses all memory of his life in Palestine and the innocent Jewish teacher whom he crucified, Claudia is afflicted by guilt and remorse and withdraws more and more into herself. She explores various new cults and religions and eventually discovers a small Christian community in one of the slum districts of the city. At the climax of the story she attends a service here and recognizes it instantly as the first scene of her dream sequence. She asks for Pilate's name to be removed from the confession of faith, but is told that this is impossible. By this time the Emperor Nero has started his notorious persecution of the early Christians and Claudia is arrested and thrown to the lions. She goes willingly to her martyrdom, marching into the arena with other Christian believers in the joyous conviction that in this way her guilt can be assuaged and her sins forgiven.

This is, of course, a fictional reconstruction of what Claudia might have been like and of what might have happened. Nevertheless, it raises again the issue of the all-loving, all-forgiving nature of Christ's sacrifice. What so disturbs Claudia, in Gertrud von le Fort's account, is Christ's look of infinite compassion as he is brought before Pilate and awaits his sentence. It is this which makes her realize that he is more than human, that there is something about him which is completely different, than he bears the hall-mark of the Divine. Gertrud von le Fort is saying that we all too often think of God as a God of justice, putting the world to rights. We do well to remember that the Christian God is one who shows mercy, even to his persecutors and to those who do evil. As we move deeper into Holy Week and draw nearer to the events of Good Friday perhaps we should recall these moving words from Isaiah 53.

> He was maltreated, yet he was submissive
> and did not open his mouth;
> like a sheep led to the slaughter,
> like a ewe that is dumb before the shearers,
> he did not open his mouth.
> He was arrested and sentenced and taken away,
> and who gave a thought to his fate –
> how he was cut off from the world of the living,
> stricken to death for my people's transgression?

(vv. 7–8)

It is this vision of the suffering servant that throughout the centuries has inspired so many to endure persecution and hardship, imprisonment and cruelty, and finally to lay down their lives readily and with gladness.

Prayer and reflection

Read the account of Christ before Pilate in Matthew 27:1 – 26. Do we too easily condemn the Roman governor? Does v. 19 here indicate that he, too, was loved by someone and regarded as precious? Might it also hint that Pilate's wife was taking more than a passing interest in the stories circulating about the man called Jesus of Nazareth? Matthew's Gospel is the only one to mention this incident. How can we account for this? Why might the evangelist have wanted to include it?

Here again, if a copy can be found, a play-reading of the relevant scenes in Dorothy L. Sayers' *King of Sorrows* might help to highlight certain aspects. Or the profoundly moving aria 'He was despised' from Handel's *Messiah* could introduce a period of silent meditation. Some groups might like to speculate further on the nature of Claudia's dream. Or are there any compelling reasons why we should not do so?

Matthew 27 also contains the sequel to Judas's betrayal, and there is a legend that Pilate, too, eventually committed suicide. Both Dorothy L. Sayers and Gertrud von le Fort see Pilate's wife as someone stricken by an uneasy conscience. Let us remember in our prayers all such people, all those who are haunted by remorse and guilt, all those who try to repress their guilt and are then haunted in other ways, all those who persist in wrongdoing and do not seek forgiveness.

O ever-loving Lord, who looked with compassion even on the perpetrators of evil, touch the hearts and souls of those who even now plan some wicked deed and persist in wicked ways. Illumine their darkness so that they may be once again brought to walk in light and, showing penitence for the past, be granted forgiveness and grace to make amendment. Look too, Lord, on those who are tormented by their guilt that they may see in the kindness of your forgiving eyes solace for their anguish, that they may know that they, too, can start afresh, and show them, Lord, some work that they may do to atone for all that is past and, with your help, go forward. Lord in your mercy, hear our prayer.

Let us remember, too, all those in positions of authority who are called to make difficult, and sometimes agonizing, decisions. Give them wisdom, Lord, as they try to reach just and equitable conclusions. May they never be corrupted by thought of personal gain or favour, but may all their pronouncements be in accordance with your teaching, that all are precious in the sight of God and that we should try to treat others as we would like them to treat us. Amen.

Claudia in the Inner Courtyard. Morning.

What can I do, what can I say
To make him hesitate and change his mind?
It's morning now, and since the dawn
I've wondered this, I could not sleep again.
I've washed my face and dressed my hair,
But always it was there, still there,
That dream,
That face,
That innocence
That pierced me through and through
And then they said 'He's here, that man from Galilee,
They say he's stirring up rebellion
And causing untold strife.'

No! no! no!
That can't be true.
For only yesterday they said
He healed the sick and cured the blind,
So how can that be troublesome?

Now that other man, Barabbas, he I know
Is truly evil.
I saw him when they brought him in,
Mean, cunning, cruel, still defiant.
A patriot he said he was, but I'll wager
He only joined the rebels as a pretext.
You could see he had a killer's lust,
A sadist's heart, a murderer.

And now they cry 'Release Barabbas!'
And my dear husband seems to hear them.

What can I do, what can I say
To make him hesitate and change his mind?
If he won't listen, then I know
Some dreadful judgement will befall us,
We shall be forever cursed.

What things do *we* find most difficult to forgive? What
can *we* do to help those stricken by remorse and guilt?

The Daughters of Jerusalem

Lent 5

Great numbers of people followed, *among them many women who mourned and lamented over him.* Jesus turned to them and said, '*Daughters of Jerusalem,* do not weep for me; weep for yourselves and your children. For the days are surely coming when people will say, "Happy are the barren, the wombs that never bore a child, the breasts that never fed one." '

(Luke 23:27–29)

In the film *Schindler's List* there is a puzzling sequence in which Otto Schindler, surrounded at that point by SS officers, watches the arrival of a consignment of Jews in cattle trucks and asks for all the trucks to be hosed down with cold water. The orders are carried out, but what seems at first to be a malicious prank is gradually revealed as an act of mercy. It is a scorchingly hot day and the people in the cattle trucks are sticky with sweat and parched with thirst. As the hoses are turned onto them, they welcome the ice-cold water and clamour to catch a few drops in their hands or on their lips. One of the Nazis chastizes

Schindler for his action. 'You are giving them hope,' he says. 'You shouldn't do that.'

We are told by Barclay in his *Commentary on the Gospel of Luke* that the daughters of Jerusalem are probably to be identified with a company of pious Jewish women 'who made it their practice always to go to crucifixions and give the victim a drink of drugged wine which would deaden the terrible pain'. They did this as an act of charity, possibly also as a token of resistance against the cruelties of the Roman occupation, since many of those about to be put to death would have been what we today would call 'freedom fighters', or rebels. Did the relief thus administered give the victims hope? Scarcely, for they knew that within minutes they would be lifted up on their crosses and left to die. But they would surely see it as an act of mercy, the compassion of one group of human beings for the suffering of another.

What did Jesus tell these women? He says they should not weep for him, but rather for themselves, because he can foresee that a terrible future awaits them. Whether we take this to refer to the Last Judgement at the end of time or merely to the destruction of Jerusalem by the Romans in AD 70, it is surely a testimony yet again to Our Lord's infinite compassion. 'Father, forgive them, for they do not know what they are doing,' the famous words addressed to the soldiers as they hammer the nails through his wrists and feet, is another example of this amazing forbearance.

On my first visit to Israel with a group of university students in 1993 we took some books and parcels of clothing from Christian groups in Britain to a Palestinian orphanage. The people in charge there told us some horrendous stories. They had been driven from their original homes by Israeli settlers, most of the children had lost their fathers in a rebellion put down by Israeli soldiers. They were understandably bitter, but also consumed with a fanatical hatred which grew more and more oppressive as the day wore on, for these people were also professing Christians. Finally, a brave young woman from among our party challenged the leading spokesman. 'But surely,' she said, 'you must remember the words of Christ about forgiving your enemies, for otherwise you will just go on perpetuating the violence.' To this the chilling response was, 'We do not show mercy where we demand justice.'

It is easy to be self-righteous. If we have not ourselves been victims of Nazi persecution, if we have not ourselves experienced the miseries of foreign occupation or the squalor and hopelessness of mass refugee camps, we can have little idea of the degradation and suffering involved and the consequent effect on the human psyche. But we do know surely that that young student, Zoë, was right in thinking that a desire for revenge can only lead to more and more hatred, more and more violence, more and more atrocities. The vicious circle has to be broken somehow, and this can only be done if one side makes the first move and refuses to participate further. Turning the other cheek is another aspect of love. It is difficult, but it is also Christ's teaching (Matthew 5:39).

There is a lovely story that as he stumbled under the weight of the Cross on the road to Calvary a woman bystander came out of the crowd and wiped the perspiration from his face with her handkerchief. She was rewarded with an imprint of that face on that piece of linen for ever. This incident is not recorded in any of the Gospels and may only be a legend, but it surely reflects the truth that any act of compassion will find favour in the sight of God. Or that it is through such acts that we come to know God more fully. This woman is traditionally known as Veronica, because she received the gift of the true icon (Latin *verus* – true) of Christ, that all-embracing, all-forgiving Love, that was then able to bring hope and healing to others.

Are women more able to forgive than men? This is controversial but many men do still seem to suffer from a spirit of competitiveness which makes them aggressive, demanding and uncompromising. In 1994 the annual service for the Women's World Day of Prayer was prepared by the women of Jerusalem drawn from the Lutheran, Episcopal, Latin, Malakite, Catholic, Armenian and Arab Orthodox churches of that city. They took as their theme the concept of reconciliation: not only between all Christian churches and traditions, which have so often disgraced the gospel by their incessant squabbles and bickerings, but also between Arab and Jew, Palestinian and Israeli, Muslim and Christian, black and white, in fact reconciliation between all warring factions and divisions. They told us very movingly about the Women in Black, an informal movement of women who stand in vigil throughout Israel every Friday from 1 p.m. to 2 p.m. to protest against the continuing conflict between the peoples of the Holy Land, holding signs calling for an end to the hatred. These present-day daughters of Jerusalem know only too well the tragedy and sorrow that result, especially for women and children, when the commandment to love and respect one another is broken and unheeded. They remind us that fervent prayer is urgently needed so that solutions may be found to the complex problems and conflicts of our world, solutions which recognize the dignity of all people as children of God, regardless of their belief or background.

Via Dolorosa

In the knowledge
Of what is to come,
He can weep –
But not for himself.

O Jerusalem!
The chicks would not gather
Into the safety
Of their mother's love.

And in that great downfall
None will be spared.
The guilty will take the innocent
Down into the abyss.

Luke 23: 27–31
Matthew 23: 37–39 RT

Prayer and reflection

Read the passage in Luke 23:26–31. What else might this tell us about Our Lord's attitude towards women?

Read also Luke 19:41–44, an earlier admonition to the people of Jerusalem. What things in today's world, or in our own lives, would make Jesus weep? What things do we need to cast out as he subsequently cast out the traders from the Temple?

If any members of the group have been to the Holy Land, perhaps a special meeting can be arranged at which they can share their experiences and reflections and perhaps show slides or pictures.

The women of Jerusalem who produced the material for the 1994 Women's World Day of Prayer told us that fervent prayer is needed so that a solution to the complex problems of the Middle East may be found. Some progress has been made, but much still remains to be done. We should support by prayer and action all groups which are working for reconciliations:

Jews greet each other with Shalom
Arabs say Salaam
And both words mean Peace!

Not far from Jerusalem
There is a small community called
Neve Shalom / Wahat el Salaam
Oasis of Peace

Jews and Palestinians live there
Jews – Muslims – Christians
In peace and harmony.

O pray for the peace of Jerusalem.

(*Together in Prayer / Women's World Day of Prayer 1994*)

Many groups find it helpful to set aside some time each week to pray the Peace Prayer:

Lead us from death to life
From falsehood to truth
Lead us from despair to hope
From fear to trust
Lead us from hate to love
From war to peace
Let peace fill our hearts
Our world, our universe.

The theme chosen by the women of Jerusalem for services held on the Day of Prayer in 1994 was *Go, See and Act*, and although these words look forward to Easter Day, the following poem also seems appropriate here:

> Lord Jesus Christ,
> you have called us to follow you.
> Lord, help us to GO.
>
> Lord Jesus Christ,
> you have commanded us to seek the sad, the lonely,
> the oppressed.
> Lord, help us to SEE.
>
> Lord Jesus Christ,
> you have commissioned us to serve the needy.
> Lord, help us to ACT.

(Bessie Webb)

What can *we* do to help bring about reconciliation between the warring factions of our world? What can *we* do to bring about reconciliation between Christian churches? What more can *we* do to act as those commissioned by Christ to serve the needs of the world?

The Women at the Cross

Holy Week

> Meanwhile, near the cross on which Jesus hung, *his mother was standing with her sister, Mary wife of Cleophas, and Mary of Magdala.*

> (John 19:25)

We come now to the very heart of the Passion, that most terrible moment in the history of humanity when we collectively, all of us, in spite of being God's special creation, put God to death upon a cross – that is to say, had him executed as a common criminal. For we must never attempt to put all the blame on the Jews or the Romans of first-century Palestine who actually carried out the deed. That would be to say that Christ's forgiveness extended only to them and that we today are in no need of it. Instead, we must remember that Christ was killed by human hatred, malice, and envy, malignant cancers that affect the whole human race, destroy God's image in us, and twist us away from our true purpose. God dies every time we as human beings fail to remember his message and let evil, instead of love, take root in our hearts. When innocent people of whatever race, colour or religion are gunned down in a terrorist atrocity, when a small child is run over by a drunken motorist, or simply whenever we scheme against our neighbours or indulge in slander, Christ cries out in agony, in anguish because we will not heed his Word.

Jesus told the 'daughters of Jerusalem' not to weep for him, but rather for themselves, for he knew that, if the world remained deaf to his message, disaster would certainly follow. We are not told what they made of this warning. We are not told whether *these* women followed him all the way to the place of crucifixion. What we are told in all four of the canonical Gospels is that there was a small group of women that kept vigil by the Cross, mostly women who had followed him from Galilee, among them Mary, his Mother, Mary the wife of Cleophas, and Mary of Magdala. These are the women generally known as the three Marys, although some commentators believe that there were actually four, since both Mark and Matthew mention a Mary who was the mother of James and Joseph, and it is unclear whether this Mary is identical with the sister of Our Lady recorded in John's Gospel or indeed whether this sister is, or is not, Mary the wife of Cleophas. Matthew also mentions the mother of the sons of Zebedee, the disciples James and John, identified by the earlier Mark as Salome. Luke later gives the name of another woman, Joanna (Luke 24:10) in connection with the women who went to the tomb on Easter Day, but he does not specifically name any of the group present at the crucifixion.

What were these women doing? Why were they there, watching the excruciatingly slow death of their beloved Master? In the Pasolini film of *The Gospel according to*

St. Matthew there is a very poignant sequence where several crosses are shown at the place of execution and at the
foot of each one there is a female figure. Huddled in their
shawls or veils, they wait there – somebody's mother, sister,
wife or girl-friend – waiting for their man to die. Their
silent vigil is an act of loyalty. It does not matter to them
that the rest of the world comes to jeer and mock at those
condemned as criminals. Their message to their loved ones
is quite simple: it is 'We are here, we still love you, whatever
you have done, and we will stay with you to the end.' It
was important that they did so. Under Roman law the
relatives had the right to claim the corpses of crucified
victims and take them away for burial. Otherwise they
were just thrown on the common rubbish-tip and burnt.

So the women who had followed Jesus from Galilee,
among them his closest relatives, come now to render this
last service. For it was a woman's duty, according to
Hebrew custom, to prepare a dead person for his or her
final resting-place. But just think what a terrible burden
this must have been! It is distressing enough in a hospital
or hospice to sit by the bed of a dying patient to ensure
that they are not alone as they depart this life, but to do
this amid the cruel taunts of hostile bystanders and to share
the shame, humiliation and disgrace of the public execution
– this is an overwhelming sorrow.

Let us look again at Mary, the Mother of Our Lord, as
she waits at the foot of the Cross. She is much older now,
almost certainly a widow, wearing the traditional black
garments associated with such status. What is to happen
to her now? It was expected of the eldest son that he would
look after his mother in her old age, but Mary is being

robbed of that security. Then she hears the words recorded in John's Gospel: 'Seeing his mother, with the disciple whom he loved standing beside her, Jesus said to her, "Mother, there is your son"; and to the disciple, "There is your mother"; and from that moment the disciple took her into his home' (John 19:26–27). Once again God has given her the means to endure her tribulation. Did she at this darkest of all times recall her visitation by the angel? It was the experience of that Presence which proved to her beyond any shadow of doubt that there *is* meaning and purpose behind it all, that there *is* goodness and love at the heart of the universe. As long as we too can remember this, then, as Paul says, there is nothing that can ever blow us onto the rocks of despair and cause us to suffer shipwreck. We may sometimes have to share a little of Christ's agony and suffering, we may sometimes be called upon to taste a bitter cup, but if we remain constant in prayer, we shall surely be given strength to do so.

Prayer and reflection

Read the accounts in all four Gospels of the vigil of the women stationed by the Cross: Mark 15:40–41; Matthew 27:55–56; Luke 23:49; and John 19:25–27. How do they differ? What might these differences tell us?

Study other references to Mary, Mother of Our Lord, in the New Testament: Matthew 1:18–25; Luke 1:26–56 and 2:1–7, and 41–51; Mark 3:31–35; John 2:1–10 and Acts 1:12–14. Could it be that the mention of Mary in Acts is a clue to the mystery of Christmas? Did Mary tell the first disciples and Luke of her experiences?

Play some of the 'Stabat Mater' from Stainer's *Crucifixion*. This is perhaps particularly suitable for a Good Friday devotional service. What might Mary have 'pondered in her heart' as she kept her vigil?

Prayer for the mothers and close relatives of people in prison.

For the Feast of the Annunciation (25 March)

A country girl.
Not beautiful.
Good bones, though. They gave that face,
Enshrined by love, a radiance,
Light from above, true holiness.

Mary of Magdala's Vigil at the Tomb

Easter Eve

Joseph took the body, wrapped it in a clean linen sheet, and laid it in his own unused tomb, which he had cut out of the rock. He then rolled a large stone against the entrance, and went away. *Mary of Magdala was there, and the other Mary, sitting opposite the grave.*

(Matthew 27:59–61)

There is always so much to do when someone dies. There are relatives to be informed, there are funeral arrangements to be made. In today's world there are death certificates to be obtained, solicitors to be consulted, insurances and pensions to be claimed, letters to be written and posted. It is generally a time of great activity, but also of great confusion. Those closest to the deceased have to take certain decisions when perhaps all they really want to do is go away and hide, find a quiet corner where they can give way to their grief, cry their eyes out or scream in their

anger, bitterness and despair. And there is always a temptation for other well-meaning people to rush in with advice
and take over altogether.

Is this what happened here? The small group of women
from Galilee had kept a faithful vigil by the Cross and seen
their beloved Jesus breathe his last. They knew this was
going to happen, but, like so many others who watch their
loved ones die, the actual moment must have left them
numb with horror and disbelief. Then, before they can do
anything at all, this man Joseph of Arimathea arrives on the
scene, produces an authorization from Pontius Pilate that he
has permission to remove the body, does so, and carries it
away, very quickly, in order to complete everything before
the Jewish sabbath. In mitigation it must be said that Joseph,
a powerful man and probably a rich one, saw the need for
immediate action, and, realizing that the Galilean women
would be unfamiliar with the correct procedures for dealing
with the Roman soldiers, stepped in decisively and carried
out the burial. Nevertheless, one has the impression from
Matthew's account that the women by the Cross were not
consulted, that they were simply brushed aside by Joseph's
haste and sense of urgency, and that only when they saw the
body being carried away did two of them follow to see where
Jesus was to be laid. These two are named by Matthew as
Mary of Magdala and 'the other Mary'.

Who are these two brave women who now determine
to keep a vigil by the tomb? What else do we know about
them? As already mentioned, there is a mystery about 'the
other Mary'. She is generally identified as the mother of
James and Joseph or as Mary, the wife of Cleophas, and
some commentators believe that these are one and the same

person, perhaps even the sister of Our Lady, while others disagree. There is also some controversy over Mary of Magdala. We know a little more about her, because Luke includes her in a list of Galilean women 'who had been set free from evil spirits and infirmities' (Luke 8:2). Among these, he tells us, were Mary, known as Mary of Magdala – a village near Tiberias – 'from whom seven demons had come out, Joanna, the wife of Chuza a steward of Herod's, Susanna, and many others. These women provided for them out of their own resources' (Luke 8:2–3).

This Mary, then, was possibly quite a wealthy woman, but she had known affliction, probably as a form of mental illness, which may in turn have been caused by some severe trauma or bereavement. There is a tradition which associates her with another woman mentioned by Luke in an earlier chapter. Here Luke writes that 'a woman who was living an immoral life in the town had learned that Jesus was a guest in the Pharisee's house and had brought oil of myrrh in a small flask. She took her place behind him, by his feet, weeping. His feet were wet with her tears and she wiped them with her hair, kissing them and anointing them with the myrrh' (Luke 7:37–38). From the context we may assume that the town here was either Capernaum or Nain, both of which are close to Magdala, and that the woman was well known as the local prostitute. Such immoral behaviour, which could have resulted from sexual hysteria or frustration following widowhood or an unfulfilled love affair, might well have been regarded at the time as a type of demonic possession (as perhaps it is?), and so the name of Mary Magdalene has come to be synonymous with the category of penitential 'fallen' women, of whom she is the patron saint. But what are we to make of the feet-washing incident? As we have seen already, there are similar accounts elsewhere, but these are associated with Mary of Bethany and the feast in the house of Simon the leper 'at which Martha served'.

Are these Marys identical? (One theory is that Mary of Bethany had moved on marriage to Magdala, lost her husband, suffered madness, and then returned, cured, to her brother and sister, but this is only a theory and a matter of speculation.) Or were there two separate incidents involving a jar of precious ointment? Was one an imitation of the other? Or were the Gospel writers merely confused as they sought to record their memories? We cannot know for certain. What we do know is that Mary of Magdala was present at the crucifixion, that she watched where Joseph of Arimathea placed the body, and that she and the other Mary sat there for some time, wondering what to do next. At some point, perhaps when the guards requested by the Jewish authorities clattered through the garden, they thought it more prudent to leave, but at least they now knew where the tomb was and could report back to the disciples. Once the sabbath was over, it might be that some of the menfolk would find the courage to come back with them to pay their last respects.

Prayer and reflection

Read first of all the accounts of earlier events in Our Lord's earthly ministry as given in Luke 7:36 – end of chapter and Luke 8:1–3.

Is it possible that Simon the Pharisee and Simon the leper mentioned in Mark's Gospel (Mark 14:3) are one and the same person?

Then read the accounts in all four Gospels of the vigil by the tomb: Mark 15:40–47; Matthew 27:55–61; Luke 23:49–56; and John 19:31–42.

Where do they differ, and where do they agree? How should we regard these discrepancies?

Perhaps keep a late-night vigil on Easter Eve and go in darkness to watch the dawn on Easter Day.

We like to see ourselves today as more sophisticated in our approach to mental illness or distress. We no longer talk about 'unclean spirits' and tend to regard reports of demonic possession as manifestations of disturbed personalities. This does not mean, however, that Satan has been banished from our world. Far from it. He is still roaming round like a lion 'seeking whom he may devour'. There is still something evil in the world that can twist and warp the human personality and wrench it from the love of God. There is still a need for healing – of body, mind and spirit. In our Easter vigil, as we remember Mary of Magdala, who was healed by the redemptive love of Christ, let us pray for all those in the grip of psychiatric illness in our hospitals and community and those who try to help and cure them.

O Lord Jesus Christ, you healed Mary of Magdala and enabled her to return to the fulness of life. You did not reject or despise her. You did not condemn, but sought to set her free from the darkness that had overtaken her. Look with compassion now on all who suffer in similar ways today and cannot find a path through the tangled maze in which they have lost their bearings. Be with those who try to help them – doctors, nurses, priests and counsellors – so that they may become channels of your grace and healing power, and help all of us, everywhere, to be aware constantly of your presence so that we do not lose our way or find ourselves blown off course. We ask this in your name. Lord, in your mercy, hear our prayer.

Mary of Magdala and the Other Mary
Waiting at the Tomb

We are alone now.
John took His mother
Back to our Upper Room,
Our hiding-place.

But we remained
And followed Joseph
To this garden
To see where he would lay His Body.

We shall wait here
And keep our vigil.
Perhaps the others will be brave enough
To come and join us?

Then perhaps all of us
Can roll away the stone.
Then perhaps we'll get
Some spices to anoint Him.

But what is that?

Some Roman soldiers.
Armed and noisy,
Coming through the garden.
We'd better hide ourselves.

For they might not respect us,
Think us easy game.
And so increase
Our misery.

Dear Lord and Saviour,
Please protect us!

Mary of Magdala Sees the Risen Jesus

Easter Day

Early on the first day of the week, while it was still dark, *Mary of Magdala came to the tomb.*

(John 20:1)

Perhaps she had been up all night, anxious and unable to sleep. She has been persuaded to leave the burial place, but she is still very agitated, disturbed by the haste with which the body seems to have been deposited, without the proper preparation or rituals. And so she is driven onwards, driven to leave the house very early before the men or the other women can stop her. Her one aim is to find the tomb again and see if somehow she can carry out one last act of reverence and homage. At this point, as we accompany her through the darkness, we must remember that we have our Eucharist, we have Easter, we have the Christian hope promised by Christ's Resurrection, but Mary of Magdala, as she hurries through the narrow, unlit streets, has as yet none of these. Despite our faith, most of us still know despair when someone precious to us dies. The pain of separation causes us doubt; remorse and regret for lost opportunities block off all thoughts of a future. If we, who are Christians, fall at such moments from the everlasting arms, how much more so must Mary have suffered . . . The dark night of the soul is upon her, the demons are waiting to pounce again.

Why, dear God, why? Why did he have to die like that? Was it our fault? Could we have saved him? Where did it all go wrong? If only we had done more . . . What he must have suffered! Why does God allow such things? There is a profound enigma about Christ's death, because by his own teaching it *does* seem to have been pre-ordained as part of a Divine plan whereby atonement could be made by God himself for our sins and for our salvation. But are illness, suffering and death always to be viewed in this way? Are they God-inflicted? Are they some kind of punishment or chastizement? Some people believe that they are, but how can such cruelty be compatible with the concept of a kind and compassionate God, a loving God who is there to help us? My mother died from a particularly nasty cancer in a hospice run by a religious order. The Sister in charge, a very devout and spiritual person, who had a special vocation to minister to the dying and the bereaved, told me afterwards that we should *never* regard such diseases as the will of God. She could not explain why or how they have crept into our world, but they are always, always, she said, a manifestation of evil, an attempt to defeat us and wrench us away from our true purpose. Sometimes they defeat us physically and our bodies perish, but even so we can be given spiritual strength to endure and overcome. Mary of Magdala, tormented again by dark thoughts and the onset of a fresh despair, fights hard not to go under. She cannot rest until she has tried to do something to make amends for the horrible way in which her Master died and was buried. Joseph of Arimathea put Jesus in a tomb and went away. Mary of Magdala returns. Perhaps the other women, woken by her restlessness, follow her, for all three other Gospels tell us that she did not come alone. 'They were wondering among themselves', says Mark, 'who would roll away the stone for them from the entrance to the tomb, when they looked up and saw that the stone, huge as it was, had been rolled back already' (Mark 16:3). This discovery causes consternation. Mark mentions a vision of angels which seems to have thrown them into an even greater panic. Her companions flee, but Mary of Magdala seems rooted to the spot. According to the account in John, she peers into the tomb again and is asked why she is weeping. 'They have taken my Lord away,' she replies, 'and I do not know where they have laid him' (John 20:13). In her anguish she rushes out into the garden and sees someone she takes to be the gardener. It is only when Jesus addresses her by name that she begins to realize the wonder of the first Easter morning. It is at this moment that her faithfulness and devotion are rewarded. She is the first person to see the risen Christ. After that nothing further can ever shake her or cloud her vision.

Prayer and reflection

Read again the accounts of the first Easter morning given in the four Gospels (Matthew 28, Mark 16, Luke 24, and John 20). On what points do they agree, and on what points do they differ?

'Jesus said, "Mary!" ' (John 20:16). Some people consider this to be the most poignant verse in the Bible. Why do we find the simple calling of her name so moving? What does it tell us about Jesus?

Later on we read that 'on seeing the Lord the disciples were overjoyed' (John 20:20). Let us give thanks for our own Easter joys, for the renewal of life we see in the Spring flowers and gardens, for the promise we now have that death is not the end and that 'there are many dwelling-places in my Father's house; if it were not so I should have told you' (John 14:2).

> *Lord Jesus Christ, who has promised that all those who believe in your name should have everlasting life, help us so to live our lives that we may continually grow in faith and, through our witness and example, may be enabled to bring hope and comfort to others. Be with us, Lord, in all our dwellings upon earth and, by the grace of the Holy Spirit, lead us towards those places in your Father's house where, in the company of saints and all faithful people, we may continue to offer our praise and thanksgiving. Amen.*

Mary of Magdala in the Garden

I am alone again.
John and Simon Peter
Have gone to fetch the others.

I am not afraid.
They say that once you've known the grip of Evil
You are always able
To recognize it when it comes again.
But here, this Presence
Is not evil.

There is something Good about it.
Like a blanket that enfolds you.
Like the warmth we used to feel
When *he* was near.

Joy perhaps I'll never know again.
Every day I'll mourn for him.
Seeing him suffer made me wonder why.
Unless, of course, there's some deep mystery
Sent to test our faith and love.

Can it be that Joseph came again?
He might have thought this place too dangerous.
Rage and hate are very strange.
It could be that he feared they'd wreck the tomb.
So perhaps he came again and they allowed him
To take the body back to Galilee.

There's the gardener.
He'll surely know the answer.
I'll go and ask him.

Mary, Wife of Cleophas

Eastertide

What is more, this is the third day since it happened, and now *some women of our company* have astounded us: they went early to the tomb, but failed to find his body, and returned with a story that they had seen a vision of angels who had told them he was alive.

(Luke 24:21–23)

William Barclay calls Luke's account of the two disciples on the road to Emmäus one of the great stories of the world. Let us remind ourselves of it. The two disciples are journeying home in the evening. A stranger joins them and they fall into conversation. They are puzzled that the stranger seems to be unaware of what has taken place in Jerusalem, and the stranger seems equally puzzled that they have failed to understand what has happened. He begins to explain it all to them. '"How dull you are!" he answered. "How slow to believe all that the prophets said! Was not the Messiah bound to suffer in this way before entering upon his glory?"' (Luke 24: 25–26). When they reach Emmäus, the stranger makes as if to go on, but they invite him in for a meal, and it is during supper, as he breaks bread with them according to the custom, that they recognize him for who he really is, the risen Christ.

This story in fact conceals an even greater story: that of the empty tomb and the discovery of the Resurrection. One of the disciples in Luke's account first refers to this very dismissively as a mere story. 'Some women of our company,' he says, 'have astounded us' but the implication is that perhaps the women have imagined it all. Overcome by grief, highly-strung and emotional, they have perhaps lost their way in the early morning darkness and become hysterical. And yet . . . And yet . . . The disciple recounts that 'some of our people went to the tomb and found things just as the women had said; but him they did not see' (Luke 24:24).

Since Luke names this narrator as Cleophas, some commentators believe that the other disciple on the road to Emmäus might have been that Mary, mentioned as his wife, who was present at the crucifixion, perhaps kept a vigil on Easter Eve with Mary of Magdala, and – at least according to Matthew – accompanies the latter to the grave on Easter Day morning. Be that as it may, she is treated here with condescension and incredulity. The man admits that the men who later went to the tomb had found things just as the women had said, but the interpretation vouchsafed to the women by the angels 'appeared to them to be nonsense, and they would not believe them' (Luke 24:11). If Mary, wife of Cleophas, one of the first witnesses of the most stupendous event in history, is indeed the other person here – perhaps being taken home by her husband, away from the overwrought atmosphere in the city – no wonder an argument is taking place as they journey!

All four Gospels agree that it was the faithful band of women who had followed Jesus and the disciples from Galilee, who had no doubt bought and prepared food for them, mended their worn clothes and sandals and washed their dirty, dusty garments, who were now the first to find the empty tomb and be told the amazing news of God's triumph over death and evil. It is to Mary of Magdala that the first glimpse of the risen Christ is granted, the final proof of his divinity and the seal for all future Christians that we are not worthless in God's sight, that we do not perish entirely as our physical bodies decay, but that we depart this life, as the beautiful words of the *Book of Common Prayer* express it, 'in sure and certain hope of resurrection'. We do not know when this will take place. At the end of time? In God's good time? There is a mystery here, just as there is a mystery about Christ's Incarnation, suffering and crucifixion. On the road to Emmäus the Stranger offers some solutions. 'Starting from Moses and all the prophets, he explained to them in the whole of scripture the things that referred to himself' (Luke 24:27). He reveals to them God's divine plan for a world gone sadly astray, a plan whereby God himself is to demonstrate that he is no longer to be propitiated by sacrifices involving the blood of innocent animals, but that he himself, once and for all, is to be this propitiation for all our misdeeds, disobedience, and wrongdoing. This does not mean, however, that we can continue in our old life without fear of retribution. As St Paul tells us again and again in his Epistles, if we continue in our old ways, we shall reap the fruits of the whirlwind. Malice breeds malice, hatred breeds hatred, lust and jealousy embroil us in their own vicious circle. But if we turn to Christ, if we listen to his gospel of love, reverence and compassion, if we share our gifts with others and help our neighbours and all those in need or distress of any kind, we shall reap the fruits of the Spirit which are 'love, joy, peace, patience, kindness, goodness, fidelity, gentleness, and self-control' (Galatians 5:22–23). The events of Christ's Passion show the extent to which evil is rife in the world, a malignant cancer that seeks to destroy all that is good and noble. The revelation of Easter Day shows that this suffering has not been in vain and that we too, if we will take up our cross and follow him, can help in the work of restoration and redemption.

Prayer and reflection

Read the whole chapter containing the story of the revelation on the road to Emmäus (Luke 24).

Why do the travellers not recognize the risen Christ immediately? Are there aspects of our lives which also prevent such recognition?

What else does this chapter tell us about the message of Easter?

Read the Easter anthems in the *Book of Common Prayer* or *Alternative Service Book* and ponder them.

'For as in Adam all die, even so in Christ shall all be made alive' (1 Corinthians 15:22).

Let us give thanks for our salvation:

Dear Lord Jesus Christ, we are not worthy to stand before you. We did not witness your anguish in the Garden of Gethsemane, we did not see your suffering on the Cross. We were not in the Upper Room when you came back to the disciples. Yet, like St Paul we do believe that you sacrificed yourself for us to set us free from the slavery of sin and enable the world to enter a new relationship with God. We believe too that, on that first Easter morning, you gave us a sure and certain sign and hope of resurrection. Help us, then, to live our lives that they may be truly thankful and that everything we do or say may always reflect your presence with us, so that your healing power may touch our hearts and minds, and the joy of Easter that we bring help transform the world.

Lord, by your death and Resurrection, graciously incline to hear our prayer.

Mary, Wife of Cleophas, Reflects on Her Experience

Early on that morning, I decided to go with them.
Another day, I thought.
Sunrise saw us in the garden by the tomb.
Terror
Ecstasy
Redemption

Jesus! it was not in vain.
O Dearest Lord, how little faith we had!
You are with us now until the end of time.

What more can *we* do to bring the joy of Easter into the lives of others and be more worthy of our calling?

Women of the Way

Pentecost and Ordinary Time

The Women in the Upper Room

Pentecost

They then returned to Jerusalem from the hill called
Olivet, which is near the city, no farther than a sabbath day's journey. On their arrival they went to the
upstairs room where they were lodging: Peter and
John and James and Andrew, Philip and Thomas,
Bartholomew and Matthew, James son of Alphaeus,
Simon the Zealot, and Judas son of James. All these
with one accord were constantly at prayer, together
with a group of women and Mary the mother of Jesus,
and his brothers.

(Acts 1:12−14)

St Luke begins his second narrative, the Acts of the
Apostles, with an account of Christ's Ascension into
Heaven, after commanding the disciples to wait in Jerusalem for the gift of the Holy Spirit. They obey, and we are
specifically told that with them in the Upper Room are
those faithful women who had accompanied them from
Galilee, including Mary, the Mother of Our Lord. We can
presume, therefore, that these women are still present on

the Day of Pentecost and receive, like their menfolk, the tongues of fire that herald the coming of the Spirit which, from now on, is to be their guide and inspiration. We do not hear much more about them. Luke records that 'more and more men and women believed in the Lord and were added to their number' (Acts 5:14) and there is a cryptic reference in one of Paul's Letters to the Corinthians which suggests that at least some of the apostles were accompanied by their wives on their journeys (1 Corinthians 9:5). Once again, they are there to support and succour and to join in the all-important task of prayer.

Perhaps it is to these women that we owe many of the stories included in Luke's Gospel. As they waited in the Upper Room, confident in the knowledge that they were all being prepared for some decisive turn of events, we can imagine them going back over the course of Christ's earthly ministry and asking one another, 'Do you remember the widow of Nain? or Jairus's daughter? or that woman who was a cripple?' (Mary, the Mother of Our Lord, may have chosen this moment to give more details of the circumstances of Christ's conception and birth. How else would we know them?) And thus the all-embracing Love of God, as revealed in Christ, would become ever clearer to them.

Prayer and reflection

Let us then remember that Christ's love extends to all and, in the season of Pentecost, consider in a little more detail the teaching of his earthly ministry and how this was later handed down to us by the work of St Paul and the apostles, as recorded in the writings of Luke.

> *Lord Jesus Christ, who by the gift of the Holy Spirit at Pentecost enabled your disciples to be bold in preaching your gospel, guide and direct us as we seek to study their accounts of your ministry among us. Strengthen us in our resolve to learn from their examples and to remember that we, too, are charged with the task and responsibility of bringing your message to others. Give us courage to share our faith, and may whatever gifts and talents we have always be dedicated to your service. Amen.*

Mary in the Upper Room (Acts 1:12–14)

I had better tell them now.
I told Joseph and my parents once.
And they believed me.
But no one else I ever told.

The angel came.
He looked at me.
His words were strange and terrible.
I did not question them
But kept them secret until now.

But now, even these strong lads, the fishermen,
These clever people, Philip who speaks Greek,
And Matthew with his Roman numerals,
Now they too have *seen*,
Now they will believe me.

The Widow of Nain

Ordinary Time 1

Afterwards Jesus went to a town called Nain, accompanied by his disciples and a large crowd. As he approached the gate of the town he met a funeral. The dead man was *the only son of his widowed mother*; and many of the townspeople were there with her.

(Luke 7:11–12)

There are two Hebrew words used in the Bible to designate a widow. One means 'one who has been bereaved', the other simply implies 'the silent one', and it is easy to see the connection. Paul, writing to Timothy, defines 'a widow in the full sense' as 'one who is alone in the world' (1 Timothy 5:4), and in scriptural times the state of widowhood was truly a state of isolation. A young woman could expect to marry again – indeed, her husband's brothers had a duty towards her in this respect – but an older woman without male relatives and past the child-bearing age would be very much left to her own resources and would have a hard task to make ends meet. The Mosaic

Law placed them under special protection, linking them with orphaned children and refugees and granting them the right to glean in the fields at harvest-time and to collect any spare produce of the olive-groves or vineyards (Deuteronomy 24:17–20). Even so, it must still have been a terrible tragedy when such a woman, nearing old age, lost her only son who could have been relied upon to shelter and provide for her.

The account in Luke's Gospel of the widow of Nain stresses the compassion of Christ. 'When the Lord saw her his heart went out to her, and he said, "Do not weep" ' (v. 13). She does not ask him to help her. Beside herself with grief, she probably does not even notice him, and in any case he is a total stranger. It is Our Lord himself who, seeing the crowd of mourners and the weeping woman, is so stricken by the sight that he is moved to act. We are given no further details. We are not told whether the young man has met with an accident or has died as the consequence of some disease. The widow herself seems to have been well known in the town and respected by the people, but her background remains obscure. We are not told that she lived a life devoted to prayer, like Anna, or that she had any other outstanding characteristics. We cannot say, therefore, that she has in any sense *earned* the favour of God. It is solely the Grace of God, moved by human suffering, that comes to her aid in her hour of distress.

It is generally agreed that Luke was a doctor by profession (Colossians 4:14) and throughout his Gospel he certainly lays great emphasis on the healing ministry. In an age when very little was really understood about illness and when crippling diseases were often held to be

punishments for sin and manifestations of Divine anger, it
is as if Luke wishes to demonstrate again and again that pain
and suffering are *not* pleasing to God and that they have no
part in his redemptive plan. Even death can be overcome by
his Divine Love. Perhaps it too is not the will of God, but
merely another example of the corruption and evil that has
somehow crept into our world. These are very complex theological issues, and Luke does not seek to expound them
further. What he does show us is the deep sympathy of Christ
for the afflicted and bereaved, and his readiness at all times
to bring them comfort and renewed hope.

There is no further mention of Nain in the Gospel narrative, and so we do not really know what happened next.
In the Old Testament widows were, however, sometimes
allotted special tasks. There is the moving story in 1 Kings
17 of the prophet Elijah being sent to a widow in Sidon
for sustenance and shelter. In a very significant detail he
first encounters her as she is gathering sticks on the out-
skirts of the village in order to make a little fire on which
to cook her only remaining food for herself and young
son. Yet when Elijah asks for a share of this meal in the
name of the Lord, she obeys him without question. 'She
went and did as Elijah had said, and there was food for
him and for her and her family for a long time. The jar of
flour did not give out, nor did the flask of oil fail.' Later
on her son, too, is stricken and dies, but is restored to life
by the prophet. 'She said to Elijah, "Now I know for certain that you are a man of God and that the word of the
Lord on your lips is truth."' We can assume, I think, that
this widow and the widow of Nain would want to tell
others of their deliverance and give thanks to God for his

mercy and compassion. Luke writes that the story of the miracle of Nain 'spread through the whole of Judaea and all the region around' (Luke 7:17) and the widow herself must surely have been one of those who passed on the good news to others and made them aware of the presence of God in their lives.

Prayer and reflection

Let us give thanks then for all the blessings we have received from God and, at this season of Pentecost, remember especially the gift of the Holy Spirit as our Guide and Comforter. May the power of the Holy Spirit enable us to tell others about our faith and bring them, too, to the Love of God and the fellowship of the Christian community.

We pray, too, for all widows and single-parent families, especially those who are struggling to make ends meet or who have lost their homes and possessions. May they be shown something of the Love of God at work in those they encounter and to whom they go for help. May they not fall into bitterness and despair, but be enabled to remember always that God will not abandon anyone who turns to him and will give us strength to cope with all our difficulties and problems.

How, as Christians, should we counsel the bereaved? How can we best try to help those who have lost loved ones in some untimely way and are devastated by their loss?

Jairus' Daughter

Ordinary Time 2

When Jesus returned, the people welcomed him, for they were all expecting him. Then a man appeared – Jairus was his name and he was president of the synagogue. Throwing himself down at Jesus's feet he begged him to come to his house, because *his only daughter, who was about twelve years old, was dying.*

(Luke 8:40–42)

Luke has now reached that point in his biography of Jesus where Jesus has embarked on his Galilean ministry, 'journeying from town to town and village to village, proclaiming the good news of the kingdom of God' (Luke 8:1). With him are the twelve chosen disciples 'and a number of women who had been set free from evil spirits and infirmities: Mary, known as Mary of Magdala, from whom seven demons had come out, Joanna, the wife of Chuza a steward of Herod's, Susanna, and many others. These women provided for them out of their own resources' (Luke 8:2–3).

Here again the names are significant. 'Mary' comes from

a Hebrew root meaning 'bitter', and Mary of Magdala had certainly known much suffering in her life, being afflicted with what we would describe nowadays as psychiatric illness, which would set her apart from the rest of the community. Joanna and Susanna seem to have been similarly afflicted and now, like Mary, wish to devote themselves to the service of their healer. 'Joanna', the female form of 'John', means 'God's gracious gift', and 'Susanna' means 'a lily' so that here are two women who present themselves as offerings to God, endeavouring to lead pure and simple lives, sharing their substance with others. Their actions may well have seemed very strange to their husbands and families, but they know that they have found inner peace and have been recipients of Divine Love. It is all that matters, and from this point onwards their lives are totally transformed.

Into this picture now comes Jairus, a president of the synagogue, obviously a man well acquainted with the Jewish Scriptures and rabbinical writings. His name means 'God enlightens', and he is enlightened enough to recognize in Jesus a Divine authority with power to help him. Perhaps he has heard about the widow of Nain, and the way in which her son was restored to her. Perhaps he has heard of the other healing miracles. Be that as it may, he has sufficient faith to believe in Jesus, even when the messengers arrive with the news that his daughter is already dead and all seems lost and futile. He accompanies Jesus back to his house, and the little girl is revived and given back to him.

There have been several attempts to explain this miracle. It has been suggested that the girl was not really dead at all, but had fallen into a diabetic coma, which Jesus recognized and knew how to cure. 'He told them to give her something to eat' (Luke 8:55) is often cited in support of this, a simple remedy to restore blood sugar levels which have fallen dangerously low. Such comas would only be imperfectly understood in Jesus' day; even in our own time they can cause confusion and be wrongly diagnosed. To the onlookers, therefore, the child really was dead and beyond any merely human help. Into the blackness of her night comes the voice of Jesus calling her back to life, and she finds the strength to obey him through the healing power transmitted through his hand.

Another explanation has been that the girl had possibly lapsed into a prolonged faint as the result of an undiagnosed anaemic condition caused by blood loss at the onset of puberty. Her age is mentioned as a significant detail, and we may perhaps speculate that Luke and other doctors had often observed similar crises in girls of a similar age. Until very recently there was a great deal of mystery and superstition surrounding women's natural bodily functions: menstruation was a taboo subject, and the menstrual blood held to be unclean. Interestingly enough, the story of Jairus's daughter includes another incident which would seem to suggest a connection with gynaecological issues. 'While Jesus was on his way he could hardly breathe for the crowds. Among them was a woman who had suffered from haemorrhages for twelve years; and nobody had been able to cure her. She came up from behind and touched the edge of his cloak, and at once her haemorrhage stopped' (Luke 8:42–44). This woman, too, had tremendous faith. She is utterly convinced that if she can but touch the hem of Jesus' garment her distressing situation will be alleviated, and her faith is rewarded.

A noted feature of this interpolated narrative is that Jesus is aware that someone has touched him. Peter is incredulous – 'Master, the crowds are hemming you in and pressing upon you' (Luke 8:45) – but Jesus is adamant that someone has succeeded in getting hold of his garment: 'for I felt that power had gone out from me' (Luke 8:46). At this point the woman comes forward, and it is remarkable in view of the shame and disgrace that would be associated with her complaint in the eyes of the Jewish law that she makes a full confession without any embarrassment. 'Before all the people she explained why she had touched him and how she had been cured instantly' (Luke 8:47). She might well have expected a rebuke, but Jesus is not angry. Nor does he consider himself defiled. 'He said to her, "Daughter, your faith has healed you. Go in peace"' (Luke 8:48).

Both stories related here not only tell us something of that mysterious Divine energy that is able to mend broken lives and restore them to wholeness, but also something of Divine Love. Jesus does not reject the woman with the issue of blood – she, too, is a child of God, and precious in his sight. He calls her 'Daughter', and here the text links us back to Jairus who was so distressed because his only daughter was dying. In a world where the father–son relationship was emphasized and the birth of a girl-child often considered a disappointment, it is noteworthy that Jairus's great love for his daughter is highlighted here, as if to give us a human analogy of the Love of God for all his human creation, male and female, rich and poor, respected and outcast, young and old. All are embraced by his compassion, and no one is too insignificant for him to notice.

Prayer and reflection

We thank you, O Lord, for all the miracles of healing that are still performed in our world, for the skill of doctors and surgeons, the loving care of nurses and all who work in the caring professions. We pray especially at this time for all sick children, and particularly those in children's hospices in our own country and abroad. Stand by them, Lord, so that they may feel your presence, and be with their parents to help them through difficult times. Lord, in your mercy, hear our prayer.

Help us to remember, Lord, that you are always there and that each one of us is cherished by you. When we consider the vastness of the universe it is so easy to lose sight of your love, but you have taught us to pray to you as children to a caring father. May your Holy Spirit come to us to guide all our actions and decisions and enable us to love our fellow human beings as you have so boundlessly loved us.

How can we nowadays best develop a healing ministry? (Perhaps those who have taken part in services of healing could share their experiences.)

A Woman in the Crowd

Ordinary Time 3

> While he was speaking thus, *a woman in the crowd
> called out, 'Happy the womb that carried you and the
> breasts that suckled you!'* He rejoined, 'No, happy are
> those who hear the word of God and keep it.'

> (Luke 11:27–28)

We are now given more details of Christ's journeyings
through the towns and villages of Galilee. There are further
miracles of healing, and the teaching ministry begins. The
disciples are instructed how to pray and are assured that
their prayers will be heard. 'Ask, and you will receive; seek,
and you will find; knock, and the door will be opened to
you' (Luke 11:9). Here again earthly relationships are used
to illustrate the unbounded generosity and loving-kindness
of God. 'Would any father among you offer his son a snake
when he asks for a fish, or a scorpion when he asks for an
egg? If you, bad as you are, know how to give good things
to your children, how much more will the heavenly Father
give the Holy Spirit to those who ask him!' (Luke 11:11–
13). The ordinary people who flock to hear these teachings

are aware that a great prophet has arisen in their midst, and a woman in the crowd is inspired to say so.

Why is this saying recorded? First and foremost, because it stresses the *humanity* of Jesus. He does not deny that he has been born in the same way as every other human being, developing from a small embryo inside a woman's body and nourished for nine months by her bloodstream. He does not deny that he has been an infant, dependent on a woman for food and shelter. At the same time, however, there is a gentle rebuke to the unnamed speaker's implication that Jesus' mother must now look with pride, and possibly self-congratulation, on the amazing person her child has now become. Mary herself would surely acknowledge that it was only by the grace of the Holy Spirit that she was enabled to carry out the will of God in the supreme task of Incarnation. If she is truly 'blessed among women' it is because she heard the word of the Lord and did not argue against it, even though overawed by the stupendous nature of her task, which was to bring her much suffering and heartbreak. The rebuke is not unkind; perhaps it is even said with a touch of humour, as an encouragement, for perhaps the woman in the crowd is barren or has not had children who have turned out well. Perhaps Jesus' words are meant to show her that she, too, can aspire to holiness and in this way be an example to others.

In the verses following this passage there are some very strong criticisms of those who profess to be religious, but nevertheless neglect their duty towards other people and so fail to keep God's commandments. 'Alas for you Pharisees! You pay tithes of mint and rue and every garden herb, but neglect justice and the love of God. It is these

you should have practised, without overlooking the others'
(Luke 11:42). Today, perhaps, we are at fault if we pay
too much attention to the minutiae of our services without
ever thinking of outreach and mission or what our churches
should be doing to alleviate poverty. We need constantly
to remind ourselves that although our worship should be
reverent and uplifting, it should also inspire us to go out
of our way to help others in the name of Christ. We need
both to hear the word of God *and* put it into action – a
challenging task, but one which, as Christ's disciples, we
must surely strive to accomplish.

Prayer and reflection

*Dear Lord and Saviour, we thank you that in your
ministry here on earth you taught us how to pray.
Grant us that today, guided by your Holy Spirit, we
may continue to find prayers acceptable to you, and
in the stillness and quiet of our prayer-time hear your
Word telling us how we can best serve you. Help us
to make the right decisions in our lives, show us how
we can best help others so that all may come to realize
their full potential and become the people you
intended them to be.*

Do we perhaps pay too much attention to the minutiae of
our services and not enough to outreach and mission?

Who Touched Me?

'Who touched me?'
Lord, you know.
I shouldn't even be here,
Offending all around me
By my blood.

'Who touched me?'
Lord, I thought
In all this jostling throng
You'd surely never notice
One small hand.

'Who touched me?'
Lord, I thought
I'd keep this healing secret
To myself – too frightened
Just to ask.

'Who touched me?'
Lord, you know
The healing that your words
Have brought. My taint
Is now on you.

Mark 5:25–34 RT

A Crippled Woman

Ordinary Time 4

He was teaching in one of the synagogues on the
sabbath, and *there was a woman there possessed by
a spirit that had crippled her for eighteen years. She
was bent double and quite unable to stand up
straight.*

(Luke 13:10–11)

It would seem that Jesus often taught in the synagogues
on the Jewish holy day, a sign that he was recognized as
a great prophet inspired by God. But both his teachings
and his actions were unconventional and upset the official
hierarchy. Here, in this incident, he notices the crippled
woman (who must have been sitting in another part of the
synagogue since, according to Jewish law, the sexes were
separated), calls to her to come forward, and heals her.
'But the president of the synagogue, indignant with Jesus
for healing on the sabbath, intervened and said to the
congregation, "There are six working days: come and be
cured on one of them, and not on the sabbath"' (Luke
13:14). Jesus then rebukes him for his hypocrisy, reminding

him that even those who say that they do no work on the
sabbath tend their animals and livestock by ensuring that
they have water. How then can it be wrong to heal someone on the sabbath, thereby showing the compassion and
mercy of God?

The woman mentioned here does not ask for healing,
but perhaps she had come to the synagogue in hope, knowing that Jesus was to be there and secretly wishing that
he might notice her. Jesus refers to her as 'a daughter of
Abraham', thereby indicating that she has equal status with
the 'sons of Abraham', the male members of the Jewish
congregation, and thus every right to be cured. He also
says that she has been 'bound by Satan', a phrase which
is much more difficult to interpret. It does not necessarily
mean that she has been a sinner, but rather that she has
fallen victim to the ravages of evil that have somehow crept
into the world. Earlier in this chapter Luke has recorded
some other sayings of Jesus on the topic. 'Or the eighteen
people who were killed when the tower fell on them at
Siloam – do you imagine they must have been more guilty
than all the other people living in Jerusalem?' (Luke 13:4).
He here acknowledges that the innocent sometimes suffer
unjustly; that we cannot sit in judgement when such acci-
dents happen to people and say that they must have
deserved it. In other words, we are not to regard such
things as acts of God.

But why is there evil in the world? What has happened
to God's creation? The Old Testament writer of the Book
of Genesis traces everything back to *our* disobedience. We
have chosen to go our own way and disregard the commandments of God, thereby setting off a chain reaction

where one evil generates another and where even those who strive to live good lives can be engulfed, ensnared, 'bound by Satan'. In particular, as the story of Cain and Abel so vividly illustrates, we have failed to *respect and revere* our fellow human beings, created like us in God's own image. *We have failed to love enough.*

Can the process be reversed? Christianity teaches that it can and that we should not regard ourselves as those without hope. Christ's own ministry here among us gave many people the chance to start again: we, too, as his twentieth-century disciples, can be agents of Divine Love and in this way transform lives. In the town where I live and work there was another old lady, bent double with age, a familiar sight as she hobbled about with the aid of a walking-stick. In former times she might well have been regarded as a witch: she was poorly-dressed, had very sharp features with a protruding nose, long, grey, straggling hair, and mumbled to herself continuously. One day I spotted her waiting to cross a road by a busy supermarket. Cars were coming and going out of the car-park, and it was obvious that she was going to have difficulty. At the same moment I noticed a crowd of young men leaving a near-by pub. They were in high spirits, shouting and singing, and, it seemed to me, looking for trouble. I was afraid for the old lady, still standing on the pavement and very vulnerable. Their leader pointed to her, laughing. Were they about to knock her over? All at once I found myself approaching the gang and speaking to the leader. I asked him if he would step into the road and halt the cars for a minute so that the old lady could cross. He looked astonished, but then did as I had requested, the traffic halted and I guided the lady to the other side. She raised her stick to acknowledge his help, I said 'Thank you very much' and I shall never forget the look on his face as I did so. All traces of aggression and mockery had disappeared: instead, there was an expression of wonder, kindness, gratitude. The other young men, too, had calmed down, and they all went away quietly, no longer rowdy, no longer drawing attention to themselves by their loutish behaviour. I wondered about their backgrounds. Perhaps they had never been properly appreciated, never thanked for anything they did, written off at school and never encouraged to develop any gift or talent? I shall never know, but I truly believe that, at least for a moment, they had had a glimpse of another lifestyle. Someone had shown them a little respect, given them an opportunity to do something useful, and they had responded to the challenge. The old lady was still crippled – this was not a physical healing – but in a strange way she and I had been allowed to be channels of God's love and all-embracing benevolence.

Prayer and reflection

We pray, Lord, today for all who are stricken by disease or crippling illness, all whose lives are blighted by some infirmity. Stretch forth your healing hand to them, dear Lord, that they may feel the comfort of your presence and be given faith and hope to help them through their trials.

And we ask, Lord, for your blessing on all young people growing up in today's complex and confusing world. We pray especially for the young unemployed, who so often feel written off by society and are without hope. Help them, Lord, to feel that they, too, are wanted and have a purpose in life.

'We have failed to love enough.' Is this true of our own lives? How can we do better?

The Widow's Mite

Ordinary Time 5

As Jesus looked up and saw rich people dropping their gifts into the chest of the temple treasury, *he noticed a poor widow putting in two tiny coins.*

(Luke 21:1–2)

The story has now moved on to Jerusalem, and Luke is about to recount the events leading up to Christ's betrayal, arrest, trial and crucifixion. Along with the other evangelists, he describes how Christ would teach in the Temple during the day, retreating in the evening to a secret place, perhaps to Bethany or to the Upper Room where he will later celebrate the Passover, perhaps to the Garden of Gethsemane on the Mount of Olives to spend the night in prayer. On this occasion, after giving a warning about hypocrisy – 'Beware of the scribes, who like to walk up and down in long robes, and love to be greeted respectfully in the street . . . These are the men who eat up the property of widows, while for appearance' sake they say long prayers' (Luke 20:46–47) – he sees people coming to offer these gifts to the service of God and watches them closely.

The poor widow who catches his attention is unnamed, but the significant fact is that he *notices* her and comments on her generosity. It is also significant that she gives *two* coins to the Temple treasury: she could easily have withheld one of them and kept it for herself, but instead she chooses to offer up *all* her money. As Jesus then points out, 'I tell you this: this poor widow has given more than any of them; for those others who have given had more than enough, but she, with less than enough, has given all she had to live on' (Luke 21:3–4).

We do not exactly know what it was that inspired the poor widow's donation. Possibly she had something special to thank God for, possibly she was simply a very devout and pious person. We do know, however, that on many occasions Christ warns us about hoarding our wealth and cautions against meanness. 'Give to all who ask . . .' he tells us. 'Freely you have received, therefore freely give.' Many of us find this a very hard teaching. There are so many people nowadays asking for our money and charitable support. Can we really give to everybody and everything? We salve our consciences by saying that there are plenty of others richer than we are, that certain charities will waste our money on glossy brochures and administrative salaries, that the buskers and beggars on our city streets are not really homeless or hungry, but merely exploiting our feelings in order to get enough cash for the next fix or bottle of spirits. But the Gospel is quite uncompromising. Jesus teaches that God sends the sunlight to shine on both the just and unjust, the deserving and the undeserving, so who are we to judge others, because we have all strayed from God's ways and all of us are in need of his mercy and forgiveness. And if God is generous in this respect and forgives us without reservation, then we too must be generous towards our fellow human beings and do what we can to help them, even if this means digging deep into our own pockets.

Furthermore, 'freely you have received and therefore freely give' does not just apply to money and material well-being. Some of us have indeed been fortunate enough to have been endowed with material wealth in this world – perhaps by our own efforts, perhaps by inheritance – and if we have, then we have as Christians the responsibility to use our wealth to help and serve others, but Christ's teaching goes deeper than that. It constantly reminds us of the grace and generosity of God. We, as people who have heard the Christian message, have been given faith, hope and the knowledge that we are loved and cherished by God. We have been granted a glimpse of the Divine Presence behind the universe, and therefore our lives have a goal and a purpose. Even when things go wrong and we find ourselves in sorrow or sadness, we are rescued from despair because we know that we matter to God and that ultimately he will not let us down. Because we have received the grace of God in this way – simply because we can say 'I believe in God, and in Jesus Christ, his only Son, our Lord' and have the privilege of drawing near to him in the Eucharist and in prayer – we must respond and give something back in thanksgiving. Our time and talents, as well as our money, are to be used in God's service to bring hope and healing to others. In his Second Letter to the Corinthians the apostle Paul says that the more we do this, the more we will receive again. 'It is in God's power to provide you with all good gifts in abundance, so that, with

every need always met to the full, you may have something
to spare for every good cause' and 'you will always be rich
enough to be generous' (2 Corinthians 9:8, 11). Dare we
trust these words of Paul? Have we sufficient faith to
believe them? Those who use their gifts in the service of
God, whatever these gifts may be, know that their lives
are immensely enriched. If we contribute in however small
a way to demonstrate to others the Christian commitment
to help all people to achieve their true potential, we too
will continue to be abundantly blessed.

Prayer and reflection

*Let us pray for the work of all Christian charities
and for all who strive to alleviate need, poverty and
distress in whatever form throughout the world. May
they always find willing helpers and volunteers to
enable them to continue their work, and may those
who live in more fortunate circumstances find it
within themselves to support them financially and
give generously. Lord, in your mercy, hear our prayer.*

*Let us ponder, too, the words of the apostle Paul
that 'God loves a cheerful giver'. May we always
remember all the many blessings we have received in
our own lives in the shape of family, friends, and
times of happiness. Let us give thanks, above all, for
the gift of faith, whereby we know that we are loved
and cherished by God and can always turn to him
for help. 'All good things come from you and of your
own do we give you.' Lord, grant that we may truly*

*take these words into our hearts and never close our
hearts to the needs of those around us.*

Should we give to all who ask? Dare we trust the words
of Paul that God will see to it that we shall always have
enough to be generous? What should be the pattern of true
Christian giving?

The Widow's Mite

Lord – the bills, the bread, the baking!
None could blame me if I kept
Charity for home consumption
While I wait for better days.

Lord, this tithe is not worth giving.
Will you mock so small a sum?
Here I place it in your hands
Trusting you through all my days.

*

The mathematics of God's kingdom
Have a different root than ours.
How ever else can two small coppers
Be reckoned wealth beyond pure gold?

Luke 21:1–4 RT

the widow's mite

Sapphira

Ordinary Time 6

But a man called Ananias sold a property, and *with the connivance of his wife Sapphira kept back some of the proceeds, and brought part only to lay at the apostles' feet.*

(Acts 5:1–2)

Luke's writing does not end with the account of Christ's Passion, death, and miraculous Resurrection. As he himself tells us (Acts 1:1) this was only the beginning. In the second part of his work, The Acts of the Apostles, he goes on to relate what happened next, the amazing process by which the small group of disciples left behind in Jerusalem received the gift of the Holy Spirit and were inspired to preach the Word of God. It is Luke who records Peter's speech to the crowds on the day of Pentecost, and Luke who describes the first Christian community, the tiny seed from which the universal Church has subsequently sprung.

All the believers agreed to hold everything in common: they began to sell their property and possessions and distribute to everyone according to his

need. One and all they kept up their daily attendance
at the temple, and, breaking bread in their homes,
they shared their meals with unaffected joy ... And
day by day the Lord added new converts to their
number. (Acts 2:44–47)

Among these converts were Barnabas 'which means "Son
of Encouragement", a Levite and by birth a Cypriot' (Acts
4:36) who sells all his estate and brings all the money to
the apostles, and Ananias and Sapphira, a married couple,
whose names belie their actions. Ananias means 'the gift
of God' and his wife is named after the beautiful blue
precious stone which is often regarded as a symbol of
purity. But this couple are not truly God-fearing. They
pretend to surrender all their worldly wealth, but in reality
try to keep some of it for themselves. They try to cheat
the Holy Spirit, but they are found out. Ananias is rebuked
by Peter and immediately falls down dead. Likewise Sapphira, unaware of her husband's death, repeats the same
lie about their money, is also reprimanded for so doing,
and suffers the same fate. It is a strange story, testifying
not only to the authority and spiritual discernment now
vested in Peter as leader of the small community, but also
to the sad fact of human sin and corruption even among
those who profess to worship God.

What a contrast there is here with the story of the poor
widow who puts all that she has into the Temple treasury!
She was probably despised by the onlookers who did not
know her true circumstances, whereas Ananias and Sapphira were no doubt admired for their seemingly generous
sacrifice. The widow, however, acts out of genuine piety,

which is seen and recognized by God, whereas Ananias and Sapphira are hypocrites who wish to have all the glory of a grand gesture but are not prepared to risk everything. They are not totally depraved people – Peter's revelation of their guilty secret causes such remorse that they die of shock and shame, unable to face their fellow-Christians – but they have allowed material wealth and possessions to come between them and the service of Christ and by so doing have enabled Satan to enter their lives.

There are two lessons for us here. The first is that a truly Christian community needs to be built upon an absolute trust in the integrity of all its members. Sapphira is perhaps led astray out of a misplaced loyalty towards her husband, but by not being completely honest both of them are cheating their fellow-Christians, and who knows what further lies might have been perpetrated, had not Peter been guided by the Holy Spirit to denounce them. How easy it is for a seed of evil to spread like a cancerous growth even among those who have pledged themselves to the Lord! That is why we need at all times to strive towards a spiritual chastity, a purity of mind and spirit, so that we do not bring shame and dishonour to the Body of Christ that is the Church in the world today. The second lesson is that, in connection with this striving, we need constantly to examine ourselves in meditation and in our prayers. Have we truly surrendered ourselves to the will of God, or are we still holding something back? Is there still an element of pride and self-assurance in our actions, a conviction that we can solve all our problems, that we really know what is best for us? We may say every Sunday in church that we wish to surrender ourselves, our souls and bodies, to the service of Christ, but do we truly *mean* this? Have we ever really thought about the implications? The story of Ananias and Sapphira is not a happy one. They are not held up to us as an ideal of Christian marriage, but as a negative example of false conduct brought about by the failure to fight against selfish motives and the notion that we can hide some of our deeds from God.

Prayer and reflection

Dear Lord, help us to cultivate within our hearts and minds a spiritual chastity, so that evil and dishonest thoughts may not deceive us and lead us into temptation. Help us each day to trust more of ourselves to your Divine guidance so that we come to hold nothing back and are ever ready to hear your word. But at the same time, Lord, preserve us from the sin of judging others while we are still ourselves far from perfection and liable to error. Lord, in your mercy, hear our prayer.

Have we truly surrendered our selves to the will of God, or are we still holding something back?

Dorcas

Ordinary Time 7

In Joppa there was *a disciple named Tabitha (in Greek, Dorcas, meaning 'Gazelle')*, who filled her days with acts of kindness and charity. At that time she fell ill and died.

(Acts 9:36–37)

Luke is a very good historian. He does not waste words by going into too much detail, but he chronicles events as they occurred so that we can see the connection between them. He tells us that after the death of Ananias and Sapphira 'great awe fell on the whole church and on all who heard of this' (Acts 5:11) and that 'an ever-increasing number of men and women who believed in the Lord were added to their ranks' (Acts 5:14). He describes how the new way of life, proclaimed by the disciples in Jerusalem, begins despite persecution to spread outwards, and Christian communities are established in other towns and cities. He portrays Peter as the recognized leader of the early Church, a leader who takes his responsibilities very seriously and who travels around to visit and encourage. 'In the course of a tour Peter was making throughout the region he went down to visit God's people at Lydda . . . All who lived in Lydda and Sharon saw him; and they turned to the Lord' (Acts 9:32, 35).

We are not given a physical description of Tabitha, but her name is emphasized as though it were appropriate. Perhaps she was very slim and graceful in her movements, truly like a gazelle, or perhaps just a very gentle person, mild-mannered and softly spoken. We have a few more clues as regards her character and spiritual qualities. We are told that she 'filled her days with acts of kindness and charity' and she seems in particular to have been a gifted needlewoman, making shirts and coats to distribute to the poor widows of the community and their families. She may have been a widow herself – there is no mention of a husband grieving over her death – but she was obviously a lady of some means who chose nevertheless to share her wealth and talents with others. There is very great distress and bewilderment over her sudden and unexpected death, and two men are sent from Joppa, a town near Lydda, to Peter 'with the urgent request, "Please come over to us without delay" ' (Acts 9:38). Peter does so, and finding everyone in tears he perhaps recalls the raising of Jairus's daughter and how his Lord and Master had acted on this occasion. 'Peter sent them all outside, and knelt down and prayed; then, turning towards the body, he said, "Tabitha, get up." She opened her eyes, saw Peter, and sat up. He gave her his hand and helped her to her feet. Then he called together the members of the church and the widows and showed her to them alive' (Acts 9:40–41). News of this miracle then spread throughout Joppa, and 'many came to believe in the Lord' (v. 42).

What lies behind that message to Peter to hasten to Joppa without delay? Surely a real sense of despair and anguish. Here were people who were trying to please God by following the new way of the Christian life, and among them Tabitha was renowned for her goodness and generosity. Why should she be struck down? Why should she have to suffer? Such an occurrence must have caused many to doubt and lose faith in the justice and mercy of God, perhaps even to question his very existence. The disciples at Joppa were very much in need of counselling and support. Perhaps they had done something wrong that was displeasing to God? Perhaps they were in error? We do not know what Peter said to them, but we do know what he did. He prayed, and the prayer was answered. He was thus able to demonstrate that illness is not a punishment sent from God, that it is not in accordance with God's true purpose. Perhaps we should see it rather as part of the evil in the world from which no one is immune and which is one of the most cunning traps set for us by Satan, for Satan's plan is always to make us deny God so that we see no reason to do anything but follow our own selfish desires and thus add even further to the destruction of God's good world. It must have been very difficult for the early Christians to accept the promise of Jesus that God will eventually conquer sin and death and bring to an end the reign of evil, and so God chooses on this occasion to work through Peter in a miraculous way so that the fledgling community does not fall apart, but is strengthened.

How great the rejoicing must have been that Tabitha

(or Dorcas) was restored to life and enabled to carry on her acts of charity! As Dorcas she has become the patron saint of dressmakers, providing us with a reminder that the gifts of preaching and teaching are not the only ones to be valued in Christ's service. The fact that the widows show the shirts and coats to Peter means that they were proud of them: they must have been beautifully made and finished, not just stitched together any old how since they were to be handed out to the destitute, but made with great care and attention out of reverence for the children of God. What an example there is here for all of us to follow!

Prayer and reflection

Help us, Lord, to use our gifts, whatever they are, in your service to bring hope and succour to others. We pray, too, for all who do voluntary work for charity, in shops or street collections or any other capacity, and for those in charge of large charitable organizations which seek to bring relief to the destitute. Help us, Lord, to be generous with our time and talents and always to respect your image in those whom we seek to serve.

'Always to respect your image in those whom we seek to serve.' How can we best do this? What things or modes of behaviour should we avoid?

Lydia

Ordinary Time 8

And on the sabbath we went outside the city gate by
the riverside, where we thought there would be a
place of prayer; we sat down and talked to the women
who had gathered there. One of those listening was
called *Lydia, a dealer in purple fabric, who came
from the city of Thyatira.*

(Acts 16:13–14)

The story of the early Church is really truly amazing. After
recounting the restoration of Dorcas Luke's narrative stays
with Peter for a while, giving us details of a vision by which
Peter is instructed that nothing is unclean or profane in
the sight of God and that therefore the gospel of Christ
can be preached to both Jews and Gentiles (Acts 10). The
story then returns to Paul, whose conversion on the road
to Damascus has already been recorded (Acts 9) and tells
how Paul and Barnabas are now set apart by the Holy
Spirit to carry on the missionary work in other parts of
the Eastern Mediterranean (Acts 13). Paul too has a vision
(Acts 16) in which he hears an appeal from an inhabitant

of Macedonia, 'Cross over to Macedonia and help us' (Acts 16:9). This convinces him that the gospel has to be taken to Greece, hereby sowing the seeds of Christianity in Europe, truly a momentous turning-point in history.

The writing now becomes much more vivid and dramatic for Luke himself accompanied Paul on these journeys and is thus no longer a narrator but an eyewitness who has been personally involved. Even so, there is still much that we have to surmise or read between the lines. We must bear in mind that Paul and his companions were preaching a strange doctrine and must have been regarded among the sophisticated Greeks and Romans in the same way as we regard the adherents of bizarre cults today: deluded, ridiculous, or slightly mad. To underline the seriousness and authenticity of their message they therefore seek out public places of worship and talk to anyone who will listen or who seems receptive. Having crossed over into Macedonia and arrived at Philippi, they do not deem it beneath their dignity to talk to the devout and pious women of the city, a Roman colony, and one of these, Lydia, is converted.

Who was this lady? Obviously a woman of substance, who had her own business importing cloth from her native city in Asia Minor, which was renowned for its special dyes. She must have been a very powerful personality because, after her conversion, she persuaded all her household to be baptized and insisted on Paul and his retinue staying with her, so that her house became a meeting-place for Christians and thus the first recorded church in Europe. It is often said that business interests and Christianity are incompatible, and where profits are based on dishonest

practice or exploitation and are used to further purely
selfish ends there is certainly cause for concern. Lydia
shows, however, how business flair and wealth can be put
to the service of God and how, by setting an example, a
business leader can bring salvation to others. It is also
noteworthy that her wealth comes from fair trading, the
desire of her native city to share its discoveries with others
rather than hoarding them solely for its own inhabitants.
The purple cloth, which was so highly prized in the ancient
world, can thus be seen as a symbol of the creative power
of human invention, dedicated here to the glory of God in
that it brings beauty into the world and thus enhances
human life.

This is in strong contrast to another incident recorded
here in which a sorceress is admonished by Paul and as a
result loses her psychic powers. She is a slave-girl, owned
by others, who exploit her gifts for their own profit. These
gifts, which we may describe as a sensitivity towards the
spiritual dimension beyond our visible world, are put to
improper use in that, by her fortune-telling and reading of
omens for the future, the girl and her masters instil an
unhealthy curiosity, perhaps even fear and terror, in their
clients. The girl herself can hardly be blamed: were she not
a slave, she would perhaps have developed, like Lydia, into
a devout and reverent person, receptive to the love of God.
As it is, she recognizes Paul and the truth of his message.
'She followed Paul and the rest of us, shouting, "These
men are servants of the most High God, and are declaring
to you a way of salvation" (Acts 16:17). It is not only a
proof of her mystic ability, but also a cry for help, and
eventually Paul frees her from the burden of her forbidden

knowledge in a form of exorcism. ' "I command you in the name of Jesus Christ to come out of her," he said, and [the spirit] came out instantly' (Acts 16:18). Thus the girl is liberated, and her owners and their evil purposes are exposed. They not surprisingly are very angry and conspire to have Paul and Silas thrown into prison. Here the apostles astonish everyone by refusing to escape during an earthquake.

The whole chapter is really about integrity: Lydia's reputation as a fair and honest trader, which convinces others that her decision to embrace a new religion is no act of madness or folly but something that has to be emulated; the slave-girl's openness in declaring publicly that Paul's message is divinely-inspired, even though by so doing she puts herself in jeopardy; and finally Paul's selfless courage while in prison which saves the life of his jailer who would otherwise have committed suicide. We do not know what happened to the slave-girl and her owners, but Lydia and Paul by their upright behaviour and example are able to bring others into the fellowship of Christ. Luke tells us that the jailer took Paul and Silas and washed their wounds 'and there and then he and his whole family were baptized. He brought them up into his house, set out a meal, and rejoiced with his whole household in his new-found faith in God' (Acts 16:33–34). We must pray that we too, through the integrity of our own lifestyles and bold confessions of our faith, may also be enabled to spread the gospel and transmit its healing power.

Prayer and reflection

> *Be with us, Lord, in each and every aspect of our lives: in our dealings with other people in business, work, or household. May we always act with honesty and fairness, not seeking to exploit or take advantage but mindful of your image in our fellow human beings and your desire to bring everyone back within your love. Help us to remember amid all the many tasks of the everyday world that we have a gospel to proclaim, and help us, Lord, to proclaim it. We ask this in Jesus' name.*

How, as Christians, ought we to regard occult practices? Fortune-telling? Horoscopes? Attempts to communicate with departed spirits?

Priscilla

Ordinary Time 9

After this he left Athens and went to Corinth. *There he met a Jew named Aquila, a native of Pontus, and his wife Priscilla;* they had recently arrived from Italy because Claudius had issued an edict that all Jews should leave Rome.

(Acts 18:1–2)

As we continue to read Luke's narrative we realize more and more that the ancient world was in turmoil. The Jews themselves traded throughout the Mediterranean and had impressed many by their strict religious practices. There were many converts to Judaism, an act of considerable courage because it brought with it a denial of the Greek and Roman gods and goddesses whose temples and shrines were everywhere revered. Judaism itself was thus a threat to the official religious cults of the Roman Empire; it challenged Imperial authority and could be seen as subversive. Into this already tense situation there now comes an even more radical doctrine: the teaching of Jesus of Nazareth that the God proclaimed by the Jewish people of Israel is the God of the whole human race who loves and cherishes each and every one of us.

Christ himself said that his gospel, although a message of peace and reconciliation, would cause dissension and strife ('I came not to bring peace, but a sword'). The established religious leaders of the day saw him as a threat and conspired to have him arrested and condemned to death. Paul and Silas, having challenged the pagan soothsaying practices in Philippi, were regarded as unwelcome trouble-makers and asked to leave the city. They went next to Thessalonica, where the same thing happened. 'The Jews in their jealousy recruited some ruffians from the dregs of society to gather a mob. They put the city in an uproar' (Acts 17:5). Journeying on to Athens, Paul had a slightly better reception and was able to make some converts, including a man called Dionysius, an influential member of the city council, and a woman called Damaris. He then travelled further down the Greek peninsula to Corinth, where he was able to establish a base for his mission in the home of Aquila and Priscilla, a Jewish couple who became his disciples.

What brave people they must have been! In his Letter to the Romans Paul records his gratitude to them: 'They risked their necks to save my life, and not I alone but all the gentile churches are grateful to them. Greet also the church that meets at their house' (16:4–5). It seems likely that, as Christians, they later returned to Rome, but in Corinth they sheltered Paul and more or less took him on as a partner in their business. 'They were tentmakers and Paul worked with them' (Acts 18:3). This must have been a considerable risk. Paul himself, we are told, was a tentmaker by trade, and probably a very skilled one, but his preaching could have landed Priscilla and Aquila in trouble and caused a loss of their trade and livelihood. Yet they are so impressed by his message that they cease to think of their own reputation and social standing. They committed themselves whole-heartedly to their new faith as followers of Christ and later accompanied Paul when he decided to return to Asia Minor, staying for a time at Ephesus, where they too began to expound the gospel.

The boldness and conviction of Paul's testimony are very apparent in this episode. He seeks out people of known religious faith and people who are well established or well regarded in their communities. Some of them are then prepared to sacrifice everything, change their whole lifestyle, and join with him in the great adventure of his mission. It is from them, as well as from Paul, that we can trace the beginnings of the Christian Church, and Paul would be the first to acknowledge this.

Prayer and reflection

Let us pray, therefore, that we too may always have the courage to proclaim the gospel of Christ, not thinking of our worldly reputations, but seeking rather to inspire faith and hope in others and bring them within the love and fellowship of God. By our honest labours in the world, help us to earn our daily bread and set a good example, and so, Lord, may we continue selfless in your service. We ask this in Jesus' name.

Are there any occupations or professions that Christians should *not* take up? Are there any lifestyles that are thoroughly un-Christian?

Euodia and Syntyche

Ordinary Time 10

Euodia and Syntyche, I appeal to you both: agree together in the Lord.

(Philippians 4:2)

It would be a mistake to think that Paul directed his message solely towards the rich and well-to-do members of the business communities in the towns he visited. People like Lydia and the tent-makers Priscilla and Aquila certainly helped him in many ways, but Paul's mission was to preach the gospel of Christ to anyone, regardless of rank or status, who would listen and believe. In his Epistles, written to encourage and support the churches he has founded, he makes this very clear. Anyone can be a Christian – Jew or Gentile, slave or free, rich or poor, man or woman – provided that there is acceptance of Christ as Lord and a firm desire to live according to his instructions and example.

In a world where people could be excluded from certain religions on grounds of nationality, gender, or social status – or, in the case of male converts to Judaism, had to

undergo painful circumcision – this was indeed revolution-
ary. Paul is often portrayed as a misogynist, but, as we
have already seen, there were a number of women among
his earliest disciples. In addition to Lydia at Philippi, and
Priscilla and her husband who accompany him to Ephesus
and later return to Rome, he mentions Phoebe (Romans
16:1), Mary and Julia (Romans 16:6 and 14) and Nympha
(Colossians 4:15). Phoebe he describes as 'a fellow-
Christian who is a minister in the church at Cenchreae', a
town near Corinth, and he exhorts the Roman community
to 'give her, in the fellowship of the Lord, a welcome
worthy of God's people' and to support her in any way
they are able 'for she has herself been a good friend to
many, including myself' (Romans 16:2). Nympha, too,
seems to have extended the hospitality of her house to
provide a meeting-place for prayer and worship.

Paul's strictures in his letter to Timothy about the way
in which women should dress and their duty to submit to
their menfolk probably arise from his concern that Christians should not indulge in scandalous behaviour. Thus
he condemns elaborate hair-styles and expensive clothes
'adorned with gold or pearls' (1 Timothy 2:9) but praises
'good deeds, as befits women who claim to be religious'
(1 Timothy 2:10). At a time when Paul himself is regarded
as a lunatic for preaching the gospel of Resurrection –
'Paul, you are raving; too much study is driving you mad'
(Acts 26:24) – a woman preaching openly in the streets
could easily have been dismissed as hysterical and her
motives seriously questioned.

Those who have embraced the new religion must also
adopt a new way of life. In all his Epistles, Paul first thanks

God that his own teaching has met with success in that others have been turned to Christ. He then goes on to expound the doctrines still further, explaining the significance of Christ's coming into the world, his crucifixion and Resurrection. After this there is always a passage on the Christian way of life, the new morality and value-system to which Christians must adhere if they are to be worthy of their calling. That is why Paul is so upset when he hears reports of quarrelling and dissension among the Christian churches he has founded. The two women mentioned in the Letter to the Philippians have been very good workers in the service of the gospel. Paul says that they 'shared his struggles' (Philippians 4:3). Nevertheless, there is some disagreement between them, and this disagreement is threatening to disrupt the whole community. What does Paul advise in such a situation?

Paul constantly tells us that we should never forget to pray at all times and on all occasions and in all matters. Writing to Euodia and Syntyche and their fellow-workers he says 'in everything make your requests known to God in prayer and petition with thanksgiving' (Philippians 4:6) and he urges the Christians at Colossae, another town in Greece, to do the same. 'Persevere in prayer, with minds alert and with thankful hearts' (Colossians 4:2). We do not know whether Euodia and Syntyche took his advice and resolved their differences. We can only hope that they did so and, should we ever find ourselves in a similar situation, remember these wise words. A retired clergyman once told me of a dispute that had arisen in his parish during his ministry. Like so many disputes, it was about the use to which parish funds should be put and it had become very acrimonious, splitting the congregation into two opposing factions. When the Parochial Church Council met to discuss the matter, accusations and counter-accusations were rife, tempers were frayed, and there were some very heated and distressing exchanges. The clergyman then stopped the meeting saying, 'This must not happen in a Christian community', and suggested that the whole council move from the parish hall into the church to pray in silence. After this they were to go home quietly and meet again in a week's time. When they resumed the atmosphere was completely different. The leaders of the opposing factions apologized to each other and everyone was willing to see the other point of view and work towards a solution acceptable to all. The period of silent prayer in church had enabled them to see the wrongness of their conduct and had given them the strength to acknowledge this and seek forgiveness.

It is so often the case that our egotistic desires get in the way of our Christian precepts. We seek to dominate others, to extend our own power sphere, to assert our will over that of other people, to draw attention to ourselves, to find fault, to know better. Paul reminds us again and again that this is not the Christian way. The Christian must do none of these things. The Christian must put others first, self last. 'Be humble,' Paul says, 'and gentle, and patient too, putting up with one another's failings in the spirit of love' (Ephesians 4:2). We should, he continues, 'have done with all spite and bad temper, with rage, insults, and slander, with evil of any kind. Be generous to one another, tender-hearted, forgiving one another as God in Christ forgave you' (Ephesians 4:31–32). All this demands self-control, not giving in to our lower nature, so that as a result 'quarrels, a contentious temper, envy, fits of rage, selfish ambitions, dissensions, party intrigues, and jealousies' (Galatians 5:20–21) no longer have any part in our lives, but are rather replaced by what Paul calls the fruits of the Spirit, namely 'love, joy, peace, patience, kindness, goodness, fidelity ... Against such things there is no law' (Galatians 5:22–23).

The famous passage in the First Letter to the Corinthians reinforces this message. Here Paul tells us that the mere practice of religion without love is worthless, for love is another way of saying that we respect and revere each and every part of God's creation, that we cherish each and every other human being, as someone unique and of infinite value because also a child of God. Thus love is never selfish, never quick to take offence. 'Love keeps no score of wrongs, takes no pleasure in the sins of others, but delights in the truth' (1 Corinthians 13:5–6). That is to say, we are to serve others willingly, not grudgingly, out of respect for the image of God inherent in everyone. 'Always be joyful; pray continually; give thanks whatever happens; for this is what God wills for you in Christ Jesus' (1 Thessalonians 5:16–18). In Paul's book despair, apathy, indifference to the fate of others are not options for Christians. The world is a place to be transformed by, with and through the Holy Spirit, and the Holy Spirit is our guarantee that we can all achieve something, if only we remain true to our task. In a world where there seems to be so much conflict and violence, where nations seek to destroy each other, where families are torn apart, where so many people are still denied justice or are abused in all sorts of ways, it can appear that the gospel of Christ and Paul's teachings, which are based upon it, have long been forgotten or rejected. This, however, would be to deny the power of Christ at work in the world. If only we could trust in this, what could we not achieve?

Prayer and reflection

Help us, Lord, to search our consciences. Are we in dispute with any fellow-Christians in our parish? Are we jealous of someone else's achievements or successes? Are we harbouring bitter or unkind thoughts about anyone? Are we picking quarrels or engaging in unfair and unwarranted criticism? If so, how can we best begin to put things right?

Enable us, Lord, to appreciate the efforts of others, in the service of Christ. Take from us all jealousy and envy, touchiness and pride, so that nothing in the conduct of our affairs can bring discredit to your cause and teachings.

What contribution can we, as individuals, make to the furtherance of harmony between all Christian churches and communities?

Lois and Eunice

Ordinary Time 11

I am reminded of the sincerity of your faith, a faith which was alive in *Lois your grandmother and Eunice your mother* before you, and which, I am confident, now lives in you.

(2 Timothy 1:5)

Paul's letters to Timothy are very moving documents. They were written during Paul's imprisonment at Rome where he was awaiting trial on charges brought against him by the Jewish authorities. Not knowing what the outcome of the trial would be, but fearing condemnation as a trouble-maker and preacher of sedition, Paul was naturally very concerned about the fate of the churches established by him in Asia Minor and wrote to Timothy both to encourage him in his discipleship and to give him counsel. In this context tribute is paid to Timothy's grandmother Lois and his mother Eunice who brought Timothy up in the Christian faith and were themselves shining examples of devotion towards the new religion.

Apart from this, Lois and Eunice remain very shadowy

figures. The only other information we have concerning them occurs in Acts 16 where we are introduced to Timothy as 'the son of a Jewish Christian mother and a Gentile father, well spoken of by the Christians at Lystra and Iconium' (Acts 16:1–2). We do not know at what stage of her life Eunice became a Christian. Possibly she and her mother were converted together, possibly Lois was one of those strong and influential women who, like Lydia, was able to persuade her whole household to accept Christian baptism. Or she may, on the other hand, have been a widow in impoverished circumstances who, by agreeing to her daughter's marriage to a Gentile, had found herself ostracized by the local Jewish community and had then listened to the Christian message as a source of hope and salvation. Whatever the truth of the matter, both women were praised by Paul for their steadfast and sincere belief, and Timothy is enjoined never to forget this. 'But for your part, stand by the truths you have learned and are assured of. Remember from whom you learned them; remember that from early childhood you have been familiar with the sacred writings which have power to make you wise and lead you to salvation through faith in Christ Jesus' (2 Timothy 3:14–15).

Paul must, of course, be referring here to the prophecies regarding the coming of Christ contained in the Jewish Scriptures. He, like Peter (Acts 2:22–36) and Stephen (Acts 7:2–53), is now able to interpret these passages in a new light. To those who have true faith in God, the Holy Spirit has now revealed the Divine plan operating throughout history and culminating in the events of Jesus' lifetime, crucifixion and Resurrection. The writer of the Letter to the Hebrews makes a similar point. He stresses that it is 'By faith we understand that the universe was formed by God's command, so that the visible came forth from the invisible' (Hebrews 11:3) and goes on to show how the early leaders of the Jewish nation endured against all the odds because they had faith and an unshakeable conviction that they were in possession of a Divine revelation. In our own day such faith, such conviction, has unfortunately become a rarity. We are assailed on all sides by scepticism and unbelief: scientific research, rational analysis, technological progress have created a predominantly secular society, seemingly given over to consumerism and the pursuit of pleasure. Can we really believe these New Testament stories? Can we really believe that God once walked among us? Is there really a dimension beyond death? Or are we just random collections of atoms in a chaotic and meaningless universe, doomed one day to perish and disappear without trace?

Faith has never been easy, but as the writer of the Letter to the Hebrews reminds us, 'Faith gives substance to our hopes and convinces us of realities we do not see' (Hebrews 11:1). It is by faith that we give purpose and meaning to our lives. It is by making the 'leap of faith' that we come to trust in a God who cares for us and who assures us that we are all precious in his sight.

Timothy was fortunate in his family background. Christians today, both men and women, must strive to emulate Lois and Eunice and pass on the message to their children. As Paul instructs Timothy, 'Keep safe the treasure put into our charge, with the help of the Holy Spirit dwelling within us' (2 Timothy 1:14). We owe it to those who have gone before us to do this. Inspired by their example, may we follow in their footsteps and be worthy of our calling.

Prayer

Lord Jesus Christ, we give thanks for the gift of faith. We remember with gratitude those who first taught us about the love of God and whose own love and care enabled us to grow in wisdom and understanding. Help us now to remember your presence with us every day of our lives and give us grace to inspire others so that they, too, may experience your love and healing power. Help us as we seek to find answers to the questions which puzzle and perplex us and which, for so many, are stumbling-blocks for faith. Help us as we strive to find just and equitable solutions to the many problems which beset our world and, as we await your Second Coming, strengthen us in our resolve and enable us, by the Power of the Holy Spirit, to be worthy of our calling. Amen.

Short Bibliography

The Revised English Bible

William Barclay's commentaries on the Gospels in *The Daily Study Bible* (St Andrew's Press, Edinburgh). First published 1953–1956

M. O'C. Walshe, translator and editor, *Meister Eckhart. Sermons and Treatises*, Vol. 1 (Watkins, London and Dulverton) 1979

Dorothy L. Sayers, *The Man Born to be King* (Victor Gollancz Ltd) 1943

Abraham Kuyper, *Women of the New Testament* (Daybreak Books, Michigan). First published 1934. New edition 1962

Gertrud von le Fort, *Die Frau des Pilatus* (Friedrich Bahn Verlag, Konstanz). First published 1955. New edition 1984

Women's World Day of Prayer, *Go, See and Act*, 1994